A REPUBLICAN
LOOKS AT
HIS PARTY

By the Same Author:

CASES ON CORPORATIONS (with R. S. STEVENS)

TOWARDS WORLD PROSPERITY (with M. EZEKIEL *et al*)

THE LAW OF WORKMEN'S COMPENSATION

KNOW YOUR SOCIAL SECURITY

A
REPUBLICAN
LOOKS AT
HIS PARTY

by

ARTHUR LARSON
Under Secretary of Labor

HARPER & BROTHERS, PUBLISHERS

New York

Contents

Preface

The two key political facts of mid-century America are these:

1. We have greater agreement than ever before in our history on fundamental issues.
2. We have an Administration whose philosophy and actions reflect, more accurately than ever before, this general agreement.

In the heat of political campaigns, it is to be expected that both these statements will be challenged. But in the perspective of political history, these two facts will stand out as the distinctive feature of our times. The purpose of this book is to show that they are both true.

The way I have gone about it is this: I have tried to take the actions of the Eisenhower Administration and see what kind of a pattern of political philosophy they add up to. At the same time, I have tried to test this philosophy by checking it with the way most people feel about such basic questions as how much power should be centered in Washington, or how much the government should do about the everyday needs of people, or how the government should act toward business or labor.

Now, it would be impertinent to tell anyone what he thinks; and therefore the only final way to check whether these statements are true is for each reader to examine what follows and decide for himself whether he finds his own ideas and convictions reflected there.

I want to make clear at the outset what this book is and what it is not.

It is not intended to be a point-by-point analysis of everything that has happened during the Eisenhower Administration, with praise for all the good things and apologies or explanations for the things that may have gone wrong.

It is rather an attempt to show forth a meaningful pattern or design, within which most of the domestic actions of the past few years and plans for the future are fitted as illustrations. This means that there will be a few important issues that are slighted, but this is because these issues would not add significantly to the pattern. For example, the question whether the Army has received too small appropriations compared with the Air Force, although of unquestionable military importance, has no relevance to political principle. In somewhat the same way, although to a less degree, most of the issues of foreign policy are in a class by themselves, and do not fit readily into an analysis of political ideas. The question of what to do about the Israel-Syria dispute, or the Communist threat to Quemoy, or the Chinese refusal to release prisoners, is not one which turns on whether you are a Republican or Democrat, or liberal or conservative, or something in between. By contrast, what a person thinks about, say, nationalized health insurance may throw a lot of light on his political complexion. And so there is relatively little discussion here of specific foreign policy issues; and a rather heavy reliance on illustrations drawn from labor and social legislation and economic policy.

This much may be said: the main theme stated at the outset—that there is general agreement on fundamentals, and that the Eisenhower program has given expression to this agreement—is, if anything, even more true of foreign than of domestic policy. One need mention only a few examples: the overriding objective of peace; the President's dramatic Atoms-for-Peace proposals; the Geneva offer of inspection of military preparations; the open-skies plan; the more recent specific offer to open a definite geographical area to mutual inspection; the offer to freeze atom weapons; the offer to cut armed forces to 2,500,000 men if Russia will do the same; the program of foreign aid, both economic and military, based on the conviction that it is in our best interests to have a world of prosperous, strong, free neighbors; the continuing effort to create among these neighbors a truer understanding of our ideals and intentions, not with a view to imposing them on others, but with a view to achieving mutual respect and good will; the policy of maximum freedom of trade consistent with our interests, and maximum exchange of persons, techniques, ideas, and even atomic materials; the policy of maintaining our military strength not by aiming at mere quantitative goals but by skillfully tailoring our preparedness to present and future military realities; and finally, the policy, exemplified by the Geneva Conference, of keeping constantly in mind that the achievement of lasting peace cannot come about solely by military strength, but requires that a start be made, however difficult and discouraging, toward the kind of understanding and communication throughout the world which is a necessary foundation on which to build progress toward disarmament and genuine peace.

Another word on what this book is not. It is not a soliloquy to the effect that there is nothing to argue and fight about any more in this country. The discussion deals in controversy on almost every page, and sometimes the controversy gets rather warm. But I am convinced that the views so roundly attacked here are now held by rather small minorities, who on

these issues are out of tune with the feelings of the overwhelming majority of Americans. Some of the ideas attacked
may even appear to be the official position of a large group or
organization, but I must repeat that the American Consensus I am talking about is not a consensus among official
political spokesmen—it is a consensus among people. After
all, in the game of politics it is presumably imperative for
the Opposition to attack the Administration in every way
that may prove politically fruitful.

At a time when the views of the Administration coincide
so closely with those of the great majority of the people, this
compulsion to oppose may drive some Opposition spokesmen
to rather desperate expedients. One of the commonest of
these expedients is to single out for attack isolated and un-
representative points of view or statements attributed to individuals associated with the Administration. At this point
let me face up squarely to a question that will occur to many
people on reading this book. It may be said, "This is all very
fine, and I agree with most of what you say; but what about
the conservative wing of the Republican Party? Does Senator X go along with your views on minimum wage? Would
Assistant Secretary Y endorse the part about federal aid for
school construction?"

To this kind of question there is a direct and, I think, complete answer. The philosophy and program of every Administration in a democracy is, in the last analysis, a composite.
Among the members of the Cabinet, the advisers to the President, and the legislative leaders in Congress, there will be
found a wide range of opinion on almost any issue. These
differences are worked out or fought out or compromised,
and somehow there emerges a single line of thought and
action, which is known as the Administration position.

There is no need to be in any doubt about what the Administration position is on any major matter. It is stated in detail in each year's State of the Union Message. It is stated again in the President's Economic Report and Budget Message. It is stated in the President's special messages to Congress on such matters as Agriculture or Education. It is embodied and confirmed in the President's legislative program, and in official testimony at Congressional hearings.

That the end product of this distillation from somewhat varying views turns out to be a clean-cut design with internal consistency and a positive sense of direction is due to two things: first, the fact that President Eisenhower, probably as much as any President of modern times, has operated from a conscious set of fundamental principles; and second, the fact that this design can be systematically carried out, because these principles are shared by the leaders in his Administration, by the majority of Republicans and, I believe, by the majority of all Americans.

ARTHUR LARSON

A REPUBLICAN
LOOKS AT
HIS PARTY

1

A Political Movement for
the Mid-Century

The Question

Is there a distinct and coherent political movement, of which
President Eisenhower is the architect and embodiment, but
which is capable of existence and growth independent of him
—a political philosophy with a clear set of principles and
objectives, which one might perhaps call the New Republicanism?

The answer here given is a plain one: there *is* such a distinctive political movement. It is deeply rooted in conscious
principle. It knows what it believes and where it is going. It
is in the direct line of descent from our oldest political traditions, yet it is quite different in significant ways from anything that has gone before.

The importance of essaying a summary of New Republican
principles is magnified by the fact that the pattern does not
fit any familiar past formulas.

How can the same philosophy urge the first extension of
unemployment insurance by federal action since its beginnings—and at the same time a reduction in the tax on corporate dividends? The greatest government-sponsored road-

building project of all time—and a relentless campaign to get the government out of business? The greatest improvements of social security in history—and the return of tidelands oil properties to the states? Increasing and extending the minimum wage—while restoring more of the power business to private enterprise?

All this does not slip comfortably into some well-worn niche like "liberal" or "New Deal" or "prolabor" or "probusiness" or "left" or "right." This is because the New Republicanism is a set of ideas keyed explicitly to contemporary mid-century facts, while the familiar categories, drawn from earlier decades, are now largely obsolete.

New Ideas to Fit New Facts

The fact that the New Republicanism is addressed and adapted to current facts stands out the more sharply when it is contrasted with political philosophies that are competing with it. Its Opposition is divided largely between two ideologies: one which might be said to bear the date 1896 and the other the date 1936.

Adlai Stevenson once remarked that there were a lot of people who had to be dragged, screaming and kicking, into the twentieth century. It is equally true that there are a lot who have to be dragged, kicking and screaming, out of the nineteen-thirties.

In a way, the second out-of-dateness is more subtly dangerous than the first. We know the 1896 ideas are old-fashioned; even their proponents admit this—in fact, that is why they like them. But the 1936 ideas are just as obsolete and invalid; yet they are constantly paraded before us as the product of liberalism and advance-guard thought.

The 1896 ideology, which had adherents in both parties,

held that business should have completely free rein, that when working people got together to improve their lot by collective means it was apt to be either a conspiracy or a riot, that the federal government should confine itself to waging an occasional war, delivering the mails and enforcing the tariff, and that individual suffering unrelated to military or public service was not a proper concern of the general government.

The 1936 ideology, associated with the New Deal, believed that private business was suspect, especially an entity known as Wall Street; that the government's principal concern with economic activity was to avert or alleviate depression and to distribute existing production more equitably; that labor was weak and needed the affirmative aid of government to offset the relative strength of employers; that the central government could, should and would create a new "economic order"; that all this required that extensive power be centralized in the federal government, and a heavy proportion of this federal power in the Executive; and that neither private business nor the states could be relied on to do a major part of the job of improving working conditions, economic growth or individual security.

There is no use in quarreling about whether either the 1896 or 1936 ideologies were understandable and perhaps even justifiable in 1896 or 1936. It would be unfair, and certainly irrelevant to the present analysis, to pass judgment on the theories and actions of President McKinley or President Grover Cleveland or President Franklin D. Roosevelt on the basis of what we have learned in the meantime or on the basis of changed facts, customs or popular attitudes. The only question that matters is: do these views fit the facts now?

Let us list a few of the many facts which have changed:

1. *The greatest change is that we have neither a nation-wide depression, nor a nation-wide war emergency.*

Many sincere Democrats have subconsciously embraced the idea of centralization as a solution of our problems solely because the Democratic Administrations were most of the time preoccupied with the necessity of dealing with emergencies which quite legitimately called for strengthened federal action. The facts have now changed—no war, no depression; but the mental habit persists. True, we are committed to a continuing high degree of defense expenditure and are surrounded by world tensions; but this should not be thought inconsistent with the statement that we have a nonwar period. It would be more accurate to say that we are doing what we have always done in some degree—keeping up a peacetime defense establishment. The difference is one of degree: the size of the establishment is many times what we used to think necessary, partly because of our new world responsibility, partly because of the greater degree and extent of tension, and partly because we have learned from experience that earlier establishments were too small. The relevant point here is that we do not have an actual war-type emergency compelling centralization of domestic power.

2. *The nature of unemployment has changed.*

While we have some unemployment, it is different in character and significance from depression unemployment. In 1936, unemployment was the result and principal symbol of depression. In 1956, such unemployment as persists during prosperity (down to about 4 per cent) is the result of special or local causes, requiring various kinds of special or locally adapted measures.

3. *The nature of capital has changed.*

Capital no longer comes principally from great personal fortunes. It comes from withheld earnings of corporations, from the large trust, insurance and pension funds, and (third in importance) from publicly issued securities. The widespread modern use of withheld earnings to increase labor productivity, and the ownership of the equities in the great insurance and pension funds by the working people of the country mean that labor and capital are becoming merged.

4. *Labor has changed.*

Labor is not a disinherited, propertyless minority; it comprises the overwhelming majority of Americans. As to organized labor's status, it is now taken for granted in most parts of the country. Moreover, while the process of organizing workers throughout the country is far from complete, the unions now face employers in most instances from a position of roughly equal bargaining strength. Both management and labor representatives, with occasional exceptions, have attained such maturity in labor relations that the expectation of government intervention can have only the effect of preventing or delaying bona fide bargaining and settlement.

5. *The idea of the inevitability of inflation has been changed.*

The cost of living has been stabilized, and in a period of rapidly rising prosperity and productivity and wages. The old assumption that there must be a certain amount of continuing inflation to keep the economy going has been discredited.

6. *The attitude of business toward government has changed.*

The SEC, FTC, FCC, FPC, ICC and dozens of other agencies go about their normal routine of applying minimum necessary rules in the public interest, with hardly a voice ever raised any more to question the propriety of their activities. Moreover, the government has learned how to use a whole array of dials which it can turn up or down to influence the course of a business cycle, through credit tightening or easing, tax actions and other fiscal measures, and the business community has accepted these moves as commonplace.

It has also accepted labor relations legislation, social insurance legislation, and various measures to prevent substandard conditions or to alleviate suffering, as normal adjuncts of a private enterprise system.

7. *Federal procurement and construction have vastly changed the impact of federal policies on everyday affairs.*

One of the most significant and least understood of all the changes in this list is the existence now of a regular annual expenditure of over thirty billion dollars on federal procurement. In spite of a considerable reduction in such expenditures by the Eisenhower Administration, the sum is still large enough to exert a decisive effect in many directions.

Thus, without resorting to legislation, but merely by insisting on certain standards as terms in its contracts, the federal government can have a profound influence in such matters as eliminating racial discrimination in employment or maintaining good wage and safety standards.

8. *The economy has changed.*

Ours is no longer an agrarian, but an industrial economy, with only about a tenth of our civilian work force of 67 million people engaged in agriculture. The theory that we have "reached the frontiers" of our industrial expansion has been exploded. New developments not only in automatic technology but in finance, distribution and industrial planning seem to make our capacity for increased production almost unlimited.

9. *Agriculture has changed.*

Although the number of farmers and farms has decreased with astonishing rapidity, production has soared, due to technological advances which relatively surpass even those of the industrial establishment. The sharp increase in capital investment and mechanization accompanying this has altered the essential status of the farmer and assimilated his problem more to that of other businesses.

10. *The character of national issues has changed.*

One of the most remarkable changes in our national life is the extent to which our great national issues are more and more centering around matters which traditionally have been thought of as local in character: water supply; housing; schools; power; area and urban redevelopment; and highways. True, there has been some federal interest in these things in earlier periods; but building roads and water systems and schoolhouses has always been a characteristically local responsibility. If this sort of thing is to be the national political issue of the future, it means that a major clue to coming political arrangements will be a new kind of federal-state-local adjustment of governmental relations. A related change of great significance is that we have become a metropolitan-urban people, with two-thirds of us living in 168 metropolitan areas; hence the big municipality looms as a political entity of prime importance.

11. *The international role of the United States has changed.*

We have an awesome responsibility for the fortunes of the Free World which must have a sobering effect on all political discussion. Wild "give-'em-hell" political byplay is just as much out of place as café pseudo-intellectualism, in this austere setting. We must have a sincere high-level honest public discussion of issues, for we cannot afford to be wrong or out of date or biased in our future formulation of policy; we must be right, or our institutions and freedoms may be lost forever.

Four Tests of a Political Philosophy

The place of a particular movement in the political spectrum is best judged by its domestic policy.

Domestic policy, in turn, can be objectively appraised by the federal government's four main internal relations:

1. To state governments.
2. To private enterprise.
3. To labor.
4. To individual persons and their needs.

Let us apply these tests to the 1896 and 1936 Opposition philosophies.

First, 1896:

1. As to state governments: definitely "states' rights," in the sense that, as against the federal government, states were the lesser of two evils.
2. As to private enterprise: deferential; almost no regulation tolerated.
3. As to labor: hostile and contemptuous.
4. As to individual persons and their needs: indifferent.

Next, 1936:

1. As to states: low opinion of their ability to produce much constructive legislation; therefore centralization favored as a way to get needed legislation.

2. As to private enterprise: inclined to be somewhat hostile, and to consider business incapable of operating without government supervision and stimulation.

3. As to labor: solicitous, because labor viewed as needing help of government to overcome bargaining advantage of employers.

4. As to individual persons and their needs: sensitive; perhaps a little inclined to operate in the mass and from a distance.

Now, let us look at the New Republicanism.

It is the genius of the Eisenhower Administration's achievement that it has merged and brought into balance all the positive forces in our country. It is not against any of them. It realizes that they sometimes conflict, but it has found a way to encourage them to work together to a common benefit.

Thus: 1896 was against labor; 1936 was against business; this Administration is against neither, but is *for* both.

Eighteen ninety-six mistrusted the federal government; 1936 mistrusted the state governments; this Administration mistrusts neither, but assigns each its full role.

What we are now observing is the raw force of nineteenth-century capitalistic private enterprise supplying the driving power to produce a steady prosperity, and the raw force of twentieth-century collective labor action supplying the driving power to improve the wages and working conditions of workers, while the state and federal governments, using the techniques and experience gained over many years, prevent harmful excesses and actions against the public interest, and make provision for the hazards and insecurities that are a by-product of free private enterprise. In all this, the key word is *balance*.

In the nineteenth century, there was not enough government regulation and not enough labor strength and freedom; result, unruly business expansion at the expense of the rights of people. In the nineteen-thirties there was too much government regulation and not enough business incentive and freedom; result, deadened business activity and protracted depression, accompanied by much humanitarian concern for the victims of the depression.

Now we have as much government activity as is necessary, but not enough to stifle the normal motivations of private enterprise. And we have a higher degree of government concern for the needs of people than ever before in our history, while at the same time pursuing a policy of maximum restoration of responsibility to individuals and private groups. This balance, together with a gradual restoration of a better balance between federal and state governments, is allowing all these elements in our society to make their maximum contribution to the common good.

The Authentic American Center

By bringing about this consolidation of the best forces in American life, President Eisenhower and his associates have, for the first time in our history, discovered and established the Authentic American Center in politics. This is not a Center in the European sense of an uneasy and precarious mid-point between large and powerful left-wing and right-wing elements of varying degrees of radicalism. It is a Center in the American sense of a common meeting-ground of the great majority of our people on our own issues, against a backdrop of our own history, our own current setting and our own responsibilities for the future.

Throughout this book, the parties to the various controversies are identified by two labels: the New Republicanism and the Opposition. It will be advisable to explain now why these terms have been used, and what they are intended to mean, so that there can be no possible misapprehension.

The term "The New Republicanism" is intended to embrace all the views of the Eisenhower Administration which are relevant to the over-all political philosophy here analyzed, whether these views are held by Republicans, Democrats or Independents. That these views are widely accepted among Democrats and Independents in addition to Republicans is common knowledge. The fact that many Democrats and Independents voted for Dwight D. Eisenhower, even before his ideas had had a chance to prove themselves in action, is evidence of this. His increasing popularity as his principles have become better known and demonstrated through actual application confirms this fact. It is a fairly safe bet that nine out of ten Americans agree with nine-tenths of what is said and proposed in the 1955 and 1956 State of the Union Messages.

Pitted against the New Republicanism, or the Authentic American Center, will be found the Opposition. What is the Opposition?

This term is intended to include any doctrine, regardless of the party affiliation of the person who asserts it, which is at odds with the American Consensus as here described. It does not refer to the Democratic Party or to Democrats as such.

Most of the time, the Opposition refers either to the 1896 or to the 1936 school of thought on a particular point. It will come as no revelation that the 1896 school still includes, as it did in 1896, some Republicans and some Democrats. The 1936 school includes some Democrats but almost no Republicans.

It will be noted that the two contending sides are identified in terms of ideas, not men. There is a reason for this. It will sometime happen that a particular Senator or candidate or voter will find himself in emphatic disagreement with some particular principle included as part of the American Consensus. Does this mean that he is outside the pale, and must be tagged once and for all as the Opposition? Decidedly not. It would be a poor kind of Center which expelled members for holding reservations on a solitary point. If this man is in agreement with the Consensus on nine points out of ten, we must remember that he is re-enforcing that Center nine-tenths of the time and dissenting from it with a relatively small fraction of his political weight.

This kind of Consensus is the distinctive mark of the American party system. It is the sort of thing which drives foreign observers to despair when they try to pin us down to their pattern, with its left-right arrangement of political status, and with its regimented voting on all issues by parliamentary majorities. In this country, we have alignments formed according to a complex system of sectional, local, traditional and interest groupings. A working majority on issue A may come about through an alliance between groups who disagree on issue B. We see this process working out in the everyday deliberations of national, state and local governments as well as in the practical business of elections.

What are the reasons for this recent emergence of the American Consensus? There are at least five.

First should be noted the common social and historical background which makes this high degree of accord possible. We have not entered this period trailing centuries of class consciousness and class warfare. We did not, as a nation, start from a beginning-point in which people were divided into aristocrats and serfs, or into rich capitalists and propertyless laborers. Of course, during Revolutionary times there were some "aristocrats" of a sort, but they did their best to play down that fact. And there were struggling laborers, but they in turn never thought of themselves as a fixed "lower class." Above all, the great majority of people, whether farmers, pioneers, woodsman, workers, craftsmen or businessmen, viewed themselves as largely identified in the one great enterprise of making their fortunes in a young and expanding country.

Re-enforcing this common social origin was a studied ideological position. The American Revolution was part of a period of brilliant thought on political philosophy. The leaders were steeped in the writings of Locke, Hume, Montesquieu, Rousseau and others, and, in turn, themselves wrote prolifically, eloquently and precisely about their principles and objectives. What with the *Federalist Papers*, the Constitution and the Declaration of Independence, there was laid down a solid ideological platform upon which all subsequent American thought could build. Unfortunately, this practice of producing comprehensive and systematic analyses of political thought has languished in this country. Communists, Socialists, even Fascists have produced detailed manifestoes and blueprints for action, and imperceptibly we have been drawn into the discussion within the framework and terminology they have chosen. We are now beginning to assert, with a sense of fresh discovery, our own rich ideological heritage.

A third reason for the appearance of the Consensus is the gradual maturing and moving-together of the interests which have provided our principal conflicts. Responsible labor and business leaders are proclaiming the doctrine that labor and management have far-reaching fundamental interests in common. The business community has come to accept a wide

range of governmental measures, formerly opposed as "interference," as not only inevitable but highly helpful to business. The antagonism between farmers and "Eastern bank-
ers," which loomed so large some years ago, seems to have
dissolved with the increase of ownership by farmers of their
own highly capitalized farms, and with the advent of bipar-
tisan agreement on the propriety of special measures to
protect farm income.

These are factors of a long-term or gradual kind which
have made the Consensus possible. But why has it appeared
just now?

For this there are two main reasons.

One is that there has arisen in the world an ideology—that
of the Communists—which actively challenges and menaces
almost everything we stand for. Principles that we have
always taken as much for granted as the air we breathe are
now flatly denounced and denied over a large part of the
world—the principles, for example, of the pre-eminence and
the freedom and the sovereignty of the individual person.
We may even have allowed ourselves at times to think of
these principles as downright trite—suitable perhaps for emphasis in a fourth-grade civics course, but not the sort of
thing you would make the subject of serious discussion
among sophisticated adults. Now we suddenly find these
familiar ideas to be our rallying-point in a grim struggle for
the highest stakes in history. A common danger has forced
us all to think about what we really think. In doing so, we
are finding that we think more like each other than we ever
realized, because the essential alikeness of our thoughts
shines out against the looming black cloud of a system of
thought we abhor.

This is nothing new, for it was also the presence of a common danger which impelled the colonists—North and South,

landowner and laborer—to find and define a Consensus with which to go forth together and meet that danger.

Another way in which this world-wide menace to our ideals has strengthened the American Center is by its putting an end to the luxury of toying with extremism. The parlor Communist of the thirties is gone forever. He affects to be hurt and surprised nowadays when the country turns on him unsmilingly and calls him to dead-earnest account, lest he perhaps still be an enemy of his own people. He explains that a lot of well-intentioned young men at about that time joined the Communist Party out of a sort of vague idealism, that there was really no harm intended, and that the whole business should be put down to immature youthful exuberance.

Whatever may have been the case in the thirties, the march of events has rendered obsolete the café-table Communist and the bull-session Socialist in this country. We are playing for keeps now, with staggering world responsibilities that we cannot escape. The smart young man who announced that he was a Tolstoyan anarchist in order to make a really smashing sensation among his fellows, or the college boxing star who joined the blackshirts because this affiliation provided him with lots of fistfights which he invariably won— these are types which, mercifully, we are no longer breeding in any quantity.

Extremism, then, is being reduced to the hard core of those who really mean business. The dilettantes have been separated from the professionals. As the extremes have, by this process, been shaken down to their true size, the predominance of the Center has become more apparent. This process will gain even greater momentum as the American intellectual increasingly applies his talents to his real task, which is to identify, systematize and interpret the indigenous American ideology as it has adapted itself to the mid-twentieth century.

The second reason why the American Consensus has now so clearly emerged, is that the Eisenhower Administration has defined it, given voice to it and put it into practice.

This point is of crucial importance. If one were to go no further than to show that a wide area of agreement on fundamentals had been achieved, this would no doubt provide an interesting abstract contribution to the history of political science, but it would have no practical impact on current political events. Under our two-party system, the decisive issue becomes: under which party banner does this American Center rally to carry forward these agreed principles?

There is no American Center Party as such, and there will probably never be. Now and then the perennial idea is advanced that our political scene would be more orderly and would make more sense if all the conservatives of both parties would get together in a Conservative Party, and all the liberals of both parties would get together in a Liberal Party. In stubborn defiance of the superficial logic of this proposal, the two major parties keep right on going. One reason for this is the overwhelming preponderance of the Center. Most people do not want to line up on one side or another of an imaginary line separating liberal from conservative. For this and other reasons—historical, sectional, emotional and practical—the two-party line-up has survived many assaults, and, for purposes of any realistic political analysis, must be assumed to continue into the indefinite future.

If, then, the American Consensus is as widespread as it appears to be, every other political question for the future will be dwarfed by the single question: who deserves the credit for marshaling this Consensus, and who will get its political support?

The answer here given is: the New Republicanism as exemplified by the Eisenhower Administration.

The primary reason is that it is the Eisenhower Administration that "invented" the successful formula, and therefore has a right to the patent. While it is true that some of the component parts have been adapted from the New Deal, as in the case of some social and labor legislation, this only serves to confirm the principal thesis, which is that the genius of the formula lies in consolidating all that is best in American life, whatever its origin. At the same time, let there be no mistake about the fact that a very large part of what is implied by the "New Republicanism" involved a sharp change of direction from that of the Truman and Roosevelt Administrations. In fact, most of this book is devoted to a delineation of this marked change. Moreover, it was not an easy change, for it frequently involved a reversal of a trend that had been going on not only in this country but all over the world for perhaps twenty years.

Another reason why the New Republicanism is properly the party of the American Center is that leading spokesmen for the Democratic Party disavow the Center. Governor Harriman was echoing the sentiments of an important, perhaps controlling, segment of Democratic leadership when he said: "There is no such word as 'moderation' or 'middle-of-the-road' in the Democratic vocabulary." This statement is unquestionably in the main tradition of the Democratic Party since 1932.

Historians may someday very well conclude that the Democratic Party was the party adapted to radical reform and free-wheeling experimentation at a time when things were badly out of joint, while the Republican Party was the party designed to carry a more mature America forward on a course of steady progress and expansion, backed by the broad support of the American Consensus.

Structurally, the Democratic Party is not set up to be a party of the Center. Its two largest blocks are represented by the most conservative element in the country—the Southern Democrats—and the most radical—the ultra-Fair-Dealers. True, there are degrees of conservatism and liberalism within the Republican ranks, too, but there is a difference. Within the Democratic Party, the cleavage is abrupt and extreme, and the two segments are ideologically almost not on speaking terms. Within the great bulk of the Republican Party the difference is more one of degree, and as a result it is possible for varying points of view to be merged into a compromise that preserves the best elements of each. The Eisenhower program, in whose preparation and execution Republicans of many shades of opinion had a hand, is the best evidence of this.

It would also be difficult for the Democratic Party to assume the role of party of the Center because a large number of its spokesmen have too long relied on the habit of attacking one part of our American life too large to be excluded from the Center—the business community. It is doubtful whether these spokesmen could ever be persuaded to give up this time-honored weapon. Occasional Democratic leaders have recently announced that they are laying this bludgeon away in the historical weapon collection. But, as of the present writing, they seem to be greatly outnumbered by the Democratic spokesmen who are determined to make an antibusiness "pitch" the main theme of the 1956 campaign.

Given the continued existence of the two-party system, then, the Center will have to express itself in much the way it did in electing President Eisenhower in 1952, that is, by adding to the vote of one party both the independent vote and a considerable portion of the vote of the other party.

If, as seems likely, the Republican Party in 1956, 1960 and later years puts forward candidates who represent the New Republicanism, while Democratic spokesmen are obliged to attack from one extreme position or another, and if some cataclysmic event does not come along which calls all bets off, the Republicans should have a strong chance of staying in power as representatives of the great majority of the voters. But if, as seems unlikely, the Republicans were some day to nominate a candidate for the presidency who was identified with an extreme conservative position, and if, as seems equally unlikely, the Democrats were to seize that moment to choose a nominee who took over the formula of the great middle way, the Democratic candidate would almost certainly win, and thereafter it would be difficult indeed for the Republicans to get back in. The Republicans now hold the Center. If they ever give it up, they may find themselves in a position somewhat like that of the Democrats in 1956—that is, they would be under the uncomfortable political necessity of opposing something that most people are satisfied with, in order to find reasons for a change of Administration.

To summarize: in politics—as in chess—the man who holds the center holds a position of almost unbeatable strength.

2

The Federal-State Balance

Centralization Is Not Inevitable

A clean-cut example of how the New Republicanism has accurately sensed and given expression to a fundamental conviction of our people is the reversal of the trend toward centralizing power in Washington.

Is there, indeed, any characteristic of the American people more universal than an abiding distaste for being run from Washington?

Let us put it perfectly bluntly: the typical American is inherently a states'-righter by inclination and sentiment. State loyalty and pride and sensitivity, and especially a keen sense of being able to handle state and local affairs without outside interference, are widespread and very real. Have you ever seen anyone put as much gusto into singing "America" as into "Ioway, Ioway"—not to mention "The Eyes of Texas Are upon You"?

Of course, the intensity of this sentiment, as evidenced by such things as singing state songs, varies somewhat according to the area. People brought up in metropolitan centers, such as Brooklyn, may have relatively less patriotism to the state than would be felt by Virginians or Hoosiers, but they usually make up for it by another kind of local enthusiasm.

Everyone is familiar with the deafening cheer that invariably goes up from a studio audience when a participant on a radio or television show announces that he is from Brooklyn.

Cold reason may argue that in many instances state patriotism is somewhat artificial when you realize that state boundaries are often merely a surveyor's line along a certain parallel and that, with the exception of some of the older states, there is no long history or unique common interest binding the people together. But, logical or not, the feeling is there; and you will run just about as much danger if you mistake a South Dakotan for a North Dakotan as if you mistook a Virginian for a Tennessean or, for that matter, a Norwegian for a Swede.

Undoubtedly it is true that there is a certain amount of good-humored whimsy mixed in with these displays of local allegiance, but beneath it is something serious and basic in our national life. This is an instinctive sense that local control of local affairs is best, that excessive centralization means the threat of ultimate loss of personal liberties, and that our constitutional division of powers between the central government, the state governments and the people is right and must be preserved at all costs.

Now, it is a curious thing that while most of us definitely dislike the idea of the gradual aggrandizement of central power at the expense of the states, for a time we had almost resigned ourselves to this process as inevitable and unstoppable. Over a period of several decades we watched, not only in this country but throughout the world, a surge of one-way traffic in the direction of centralization of authority and strengthening of the Executive. At the end of this road, in many countries, was totalitarian dictatorship. Everyone from science-fiction writers to political scientists seemed to assume that it was only a matter of time until all countries must be dominated by a powerful central executive. Has it ever struck you that writers who describe how life will be in 1984 or 2000, for such purposes as interplanetary television shows or political satires or comic strips, whatever their other disagreements always seem to agree on one thing: the political arrangements of the future will consist of one or more centralized dictatorships—maybe a "Big Brother," maybe a scientist with a colossal head bulging beneath his space helmet, maybe a strong-willed but ravishing blonde dressed in well-tailored cellophane coveralls—but always a central dictatorship.

This assumption of the inevitability of centralization is particularly prevalent among younger people, although it should not be attributed to the influence of comic books and television. (Those two media are blamed for enough things without adding this to the list.) The real reason is that young people have spent most of their lives in a period which witnessed a consistent extension of federal government activity over a span of twenty years. This extension was called forth, first, by a nation-wide depression, and then by the Second World War and the Korean conflict. If you jotted down on graph paper the dots showing higher and higher federal government participation and intervention in all phases of life, and then drew a line between them and projected the line into the future, you would quite probably see nothing ahead but a withering-away of state and local government and a relentless accretion of authority to Washington.

No one is disposed to argue with the obvious explanation, which is that grave nation-wide emergencies, whether of war or depression, quite legitimately demand a greatly heightened assumption of responsibility by the central authority. If there had been no more to the story than this, the matter of state-federal division of function would not have become a major national issue.

The trouble was that those who had acquired a taste for centralized power as a result of assuming it for valid emergency purposes did not want to give it back when the emergency was over.

To put it another way: the habit of doing more and more things from Washington became so fixed during a period when a good reason existed that the habit could not be broken when the reason disappeared.

In addition, we must recognize that these "centralizers" were under the influence of a school of European political theory which emphatically argued that any modern country requires a strong central Executive which wields the ultimate power. The late Professor Harold Laski was a well-known advocate of this theory, and, in his book *The American Presidency,* he specifically argued for its application in the United States. The corollary of this taste for centralization is a thinly veiled contempt for state and municipal government, which may be betrayed by the choice of a phrase, as in the following passage from Mr. Dean Acheson's book, *A Democrat Looks at His Party:* "The [Republican] party historically would subordinate . . . the national voice to a babel of local voices."

The Eisenhower Administration, in common with the American public, not only disagreed with this theory of the desirability of centralization, but also recognized that in this period of prosperity and relative peace we had a chance to work out an adaptation of our traditional state-federal relation to the needs of today, if we would only take it.

No time was lost in translating this belief into action. One of the first steps was the reduction of the size of the federal establishment by several hundred thousand positions. You may call it coincidence if you like—but the number of people on other government payrolls increased by almost the exact amount of the decrease in federal government personnel.

A considered policy was announced under which the central government would undertake to do only those things which the states or the people could not do for themselves. An exhaustive analysis with detailed recommendations was made by a specially created Commission on Intergovernmental Relations.

At the same time, assisting the building up of the quality, prestige, fiscal strength and responsibility of state and local governments was made a specific federal government objective. President Eisenhower summed up both the policy and the reason in a statement to the Governors' Conference in Seattle, Washington, on August 4, 1953:

I am here for a very simple purpose, because of my indestructible conviction that unless we preserve in this country the place of the state government, its traditional place—with the power, the authority, and the revenue necessary to discharge those responsibilities—then we are not going to have an America as we have known it. We will have some other form of government.

Determining the Division of Function

Our traditional state-federal relation, we must never forget, starts with a general presumption in favor of state and individual rights, under the constitutional concept that the powers not granted to the federal government are reserved to the states or to the people.

As a practical matter, there are two main tests that guide the decision on how widely federal activities should range.

The first is the question of ability to do the particular job, and second is the question of legitimate national interest in the problem.

As to the first: there are many tasks of such size and scope that they can only be undertaken nationally. They include such familiar functions of the federal government as conduct of foreign and military affairs, immigration and national security activities. But they also include newer functions, necessitated both by changed conditions and by the changed attitudes and expectations of the people. As these new items come along, it is necessary constantly to apply the simple two-part test: is this something that needs to be done, and, if so, is it the sort of thing that only the federal government can successfully do? And so, without much argument, we find the federal government doing such things as developing atomic energy both for peaceful uses and for weapons, looking after certain national resources, and carrying out programs of flood control that would be beyond the capacity of any state. We also find that the federal government recognizes a continuing responsibility for averting nation-wide depression.

But there is a second question also: to what extent does the national authority have a legitimate interest in a particular aspect of our lives? Assume it can find the constitutional and legal power, and assume it is the only agency which, for practical, administrative and financial reasons, can handle the problem—is it any of the central government's business to worry about, for example, child labor or minimum wages or a drought in Texas?

There was a drought in Texas in 1887, and President Grover Cleveland responded to the situation by vetoing a bill to distribute seeds to the drought-stricken farmers, saying: "I do not believe that the power and duty of the General

Government ought to be extended to the relief of individual suffering which is in no manner properly related to the public service or benefit."

We have come a long way since Grover Cleveland. When Texas once more was visited by drought, in 1953 and 1954, the federal government stepped in with Public Law 875, the President's Disaster Relief Fund, its program of providing feed at a discount for basic herds, its hay transportation program, its special livestock loans and so on.

We have, as a people, evolved a pretty clear philosophy on this point. Thus, our traditions of individualism dictate that our people should be free to conduct their business affairs as they choose within a very wide range. But these same traditions of individual worth also dictate a limit on this range: when the free play of business or economic forces has the effect of grinding down a fellow human being into a condition which affronts our concept of decency, the power of the general government stands ready to blot out these substandard conditions. That is why we have such things as minimum wage laws and child labor laws.

There is another legitimate ground for federal concern which must never be overlooked. We live in an era which forces upon the central government a continuing and grave responsibility for national security. This means that it must assume an interest in some matters, such as loss of manpower resources through injury, lack of training or discrimination, that might at one time have been thought to be of exclusively private or local interest.

The Emerging Federal-State Pattern

How does one reconcile this broad concept of the legitimate interests of government with the studied policy of cutting down centralized control?

The answer is that, when the federal government elects to refrain from actual control of some area of important activity, it does so not with the idea of leaving a vacuum, but with the idea that the job should and will be done by state, local or private efforts. It follows that the success of this approach will be in proportion to the willingness and ability of the states and private groups to assume this responsibility.

Lawyers are familiar with the Hohfeldian concept that for every right there is a corresponding duty. So it is here. Whenever we speak of states' rights, we should never forget to add that there go with those rights the corresponding states' responsibilities. As Elihu Root said many years ago: "If the powers of the States are to be preserved and their authority is to continue, the States must exercise their powers. The only way to maintain the powers of Government is to govern."

The states have indeed been making progress in the assumption of this kind of responsibility. Obsolete state constitutions are being revised. More municipal home rule and greatly improved municipal organization can be observed. Court systems are being simplified and modernized, as are also state executive agencies. Salaries are being raised, and more competent men are being brought into legislatures and other branches of state public service. Improvements are also being made in school systems, mental health facilities, training-research programs, child guidance clinics, rehabilitation centers, highway systems, conservation, civil service, housing and health services, agricultural activities, elections, judicial reform and many other fields.

The essential thing, then, if we are going to meet the challenge of discharging the manifold modern responsibilities of government without succumbing to the temptation of excessive centralization, is that we bend every effort to make state governments, state agencies and state legislation more effective.

There are many ways this can be done and is being done.

The primary responsibility, of course, rests with the citizens of the state. The times call for a redoubled public interest in state government and legislation.

A reason often given for the necessity for central action is the fact that a particular problem crosses state lines. Thanks to a promising new technique, this reason can be overcome in many cases. The new technique is known as an Interstate Compact. These are simply agreements between two or more states, pursuant to federal enabling legislation to take care of any jurisdictional question, under which the states work out some common difficulty or carry on some useful activity affecting more than one state. The constitutionality of these compacts has been upheld, and they have recently been held by the Supreme Court to be binding on succeeding legislatures, in a compact involving pollution control. Other compacts, either ratified or authorized, have dealt with control and supervision of water resources in the Great Lakes region, forest fire protection in the Southeast, fishing in the Colorado River, and waterfront crime in the New York–New Jersey dock area.

Another reason sometimes advanced for centralization is the desirability of uniformity throughout the country, as, for example, in the case of laws governing commercial transactions. Here again there is a technique available, which has been successful in a number of fields and could be extended. It is the working-out and adoption of uniform laws by states and by groups such as the American Law Institute and the Commission on Uniform State Laws.

As far as the federal government is concerned, there is a great deal it can do to contribute toward the effectiveness of state governments, without becoming actually involved in direct everyday control of a program.

One method has been the grant-in-aid device, which has been used for slum clearance, civil defense, public assistance, public health, education, rehabilitation and so on, in amounts exceeding two billion dollars annually. The grant-in-aid mechanism, under which the federal government typically agrees to supply funds to finance a state-operated activity on condition that the activity meet certain broad standards and, usually, that the state itself supply a specified proportion of the necessary funds, has admittedly led to some frictions in the past. State officials sometimes are inclined to feel that the "feds" are breathing too closely down their necks; the federal government officials, in turn, wish the state people would acquire a more sympathetic realization of the fact that the federal government cannot just hand over large sums of money without some idea of what happens to the money thereafter. These occasional strains have obscured the main fact, which is that, properly conceived and administered, a grant-in-aid system can not only bring about a worth-while public service, but also in the process greatly enhance the strength and quality of state government. A strong, well-financed department is set up; high personnel standards are established; and as the citizens of the state observe the state government doing a good job on more and more important governmental assignments the respect of the people for their state government rises. If such a partnership is to work smoothly, however, every administrator on both sides has to be imbued with the kind of balanced philosophy of federal-state relations that the American Consensus calls for. An adherent of Laski's dominant-central-executive theory could hardly be expected to fit harmoniously into this kind of relation.

There are many other ways in which the federal government can contribute to the improvement of state laws and activities without unseemly interference. Although it does not seem to be widely known, there is a large volume of everyday activity among federal agencies in the form of technical assistance to states in preparing legislation, assistance with organizing and planning programs, and actual help on drafting of laws. The central government is well situated to act as a pool or clearinghouse for the best experience of the several states, and to provide such useful services as, for example, the training of safety personnel.

Even moral support and encouragement can sometimes help a state toward better laws. For example, President Eisenhower and Secretary of Labor Mitchell made a special effort, in such places as the State of the Union Message, the Economic Report, letters to Governors, speeches and conferences, to urge the states to raise the standards of their unemployment insurance and workmen's compensation laws. In 1955 forty-five states amended these laws, in most instances with an increase in benefits. It was the greatest burst of activity in this area since these systems were completed, and it certainly seems to confirm the conclusion that the state governments are quite willing and able to respond with enthusiasm to a policy of rebuilding state responsibility.

Another move in this direction is improved communications with the states and a feeling that the states and the federal government are working together in a joint venture relationship. Conferences with the Governors, systematic liaison with the Council of State Governments, frequent meetings with state officials and legislative representatives, and the free and constant exchange of ideas throughout the year are all helping toward this objective.

Whenever possible, the federal government is trying to handle projects on a federal-state partnership arrangement, rather than as purely federal enterprises. This is true, for example, in the case of reclamation projects, water-power resources development, highways, soil conservation and community redevelopment.

Similarly, the federal government makes a contribution to the strength and prestige of state governments and agencies by delegating to the states portions of its own programs. For example, when the Eisenhower Administration's plan of unemployment insurance for federal workers was adopted, the legislation did not—as it easily could have done—set up a separate federal system with federal administration. Rather, it provided that federal employees should be paid benefits according to state laws, under regular state administration, with the federal government reimbursing the states for the outlay. Again, the task of determining existence of disability for purposes of the Eisenhower Administration's "disability freeze" under the old-age and survivors insurance program was farmed out to state agencies, rather than being done by the addition of more federal offices and employees.

Moreover, the federal government can set a good example in those areas where it has direct operating responsibility. Accordingly, as shown later in Chapter 4, an unprecedented effort has been made to better the legislation applicable to the District of Columbia and to federal employees.

One special application of the over-all policy—the return of tidelands oil properties to the states—deserves special attention because the very violence of the controversy that surrounded the move highlights the contrasting philosophies that were at stake.

The beginning-point of the tidelands oil story is this: the right of the states to the offshore areas involved had been affirmed in 30 rulings of the federal government's own Department of Interior, 244 rulings of various federal and state courts, and 53 decisions of the Supreme Court of the United States. At least one state had once tried to give these lands to the federal government and the federal government had refused to accept the gift.

Now, while political theory and the exigencies of the modern world have been gradually enlarging the powers of the central government, as described above, a parallel process has been going on in legal and constitutional theory to accommodate these new developments.

And so, in 1947, it happened that the Supreme Court handed down a decision awarding the offshore lands—which by now had acquired considerable value due to their oil-bearing potentialities—to the federal government.

During the 1952 campaign, Mr. Eisenhower promised that, if elected, he would sponsor the return of the tidelands to the states, and appropriate legislation was enacted early in his Administration.

One will not soon forget the vehemence of attack which was leveled at this promise and its fulfillment, coming from the most vocal partisans of centralization. Oddly, the theme of the attack was that this was a "giveaway" by the people. The truth was that it was nothing of the sort; it was a transfer by the people (as federal government) to the people (as state government). Lurking behind this "giveaway" theme was sometimes a sinister hint that the state governments involved were so corrupt that giving anything to them was equivalent to giving it to a few big private business interests. One cannot help pausing at this point to observe that a school of thought which holds this low an opinion of the integrity of state governments can hardly, if left to itself, be expected to leave much in the long run of the state share of the federal-state balance of functions contemplated by the framers of our Constitution.

Another argument against the return of these lands was the very blunt statement, having nothing to do with political theory, that the federal government had a lot of places where it could use income from these properties, and that this income would lighten federal taxation. The same statement, of course, could be made of the states, which leaves this line of argument at a standoff. What is more important is that an indispensable component of the over-all process of strengthening state government is the strengthening of the independent sources of revenue available to the states. True, only a few states were involved here; but this does not change the principle that, other things being equal, priority should be given to the tax problem of the states, which in most instances is even more difficult than the tax problem of the federal government.

The net result of the move was to stimulate development of a new and rich source of oil on the Continental Shelf, to the benefit alike of the states (which charge as much as twenty dollars an acre for exploration, compared with the federal rate of fifty cents for unproved land, and royalties of 12½ per cent or more compared with federal royalty rates of as low as 5 per cent), the federal government, which profits by new sources of tax revenue, and the thousands of workers who are given employment.

Ultimate Objective: the Individual Person

At this point, it may be said, "All these efforts toward getting the desired result through building up more effective state governments are quite impressive and interesting; but, to return to the initial question, why go to all that bother? What's wrong with centralization anyway?"

This is not a question that can be answered with statistics. The values at stake are largely intangible, and the arguments are probably not susceptible of absolute proof. Fortunately for those who believe in the importance of avoiding centralization, the vast majority of Americans instinctively sense these values and these arguments, and, deep in their hearts, know that great concentration of power is an evil and dangerous thing without having to have it proved to them.

What lies behind this conviction? Basically, it is an intuitive knowledge that, sooner or later, the accumulation of power in a central government leads to a loss of the freedom, enterprise and importance of the individual person.

If we want to look abroad, there is plenty of evidence supporting this conviction. Once power is concentrated, even for beneficent purposes, it is all there in one package where it can be grabbed by those whose purposes are not beneficent at all. But if power is diffused, in a pluralistic society such as ours, this cannot happen. Every schoolboy knows this is why the founders of our country carefully divided power between the state and federal levels. Nothing has happened in the meantime to call in question the validity of this arrangement; in fact, the succession of absolutisms which we have witnessed in countries lacking this kind of separation is strong confirmation of the inspired wisdom of those who gave our political structure its enduring form.

The more pluralistic a society is, the more difficult it is for any form of totalitarianism to take it over. It is therefore standard order of procedure in established Communist strategy, precisely as it was in Hitler's strategy, to prepare the ground for absolutism by systematically corrupting, discrediting and destroying all allegiances, all sources of authority in everyday life, and all the ties or associations that are a familiar feature of a pluralistic society. In this kind of calculated

campaign, all regional or local political entities must be
sharply brought to heel; the churches and religion must be
defiled and if possible destroyed; the authority of the family
itself must be undermined; and then attention can be given
to the multitude of lesser loyalties—the hiking club, the singing society, the university, the business corporation, the fraternal society, the union. Once this job of demolition is
well advanced, the second phase can be undertaken: into
the vacuum thus created is introduced the One Authority,
the One Loyalty. There will be recreational clubs again—but
in the form of a Strength through Joy organization emanat-
ing directly from The Leader, for which everyone must be
everlastingly grateful to The Leader. In place of the other
social and fraternal ties, there will be the uniformed bands of
Hitler Youth. All lines of authority must proceed forth from
the central Communist or Fascist repository of power; all
lines of loyalty must return back along the same lines to the
central object of faith and gratitude.

We never appreciate, until we view ourselves in contrast
with a modern totalitarian establishment, what a bewildering
variety of organizations, large and small, exercise some little
fragment of authority over us, and command some little fraction of our devotion. Governmental authority alone is divided
and subdivided in many directions: the national level, divided in turn into legislative, judicial and executive branches;
the state level, similarly divided; county government; municipal government; school boards; irrigation districts; port
authorities—the list could go on and on. Then there are all
the nongovernmental sources of authority: churches, church
organizations, social clubs, lodges, trade unions, trade associations, corporations, colleges, alumni associations, ski clubs,
bar associations, Ladies' Aids, civic theater groups. Sometimes the authority is very slight: for example, the right of

the Barber Shop Quartet Society to require you to attend practices and pay dues, or to expel you if you disobey. Sometimes the authority is great: for example, the power of some professional associations to regulate their members' behavior and virtually to destroy an offender's livelihood.

Once we appreciate that our strength against the world trend toward totalitarianism lies in this very diffusion of power and loyalty, we will be keenly sensitive to any development that threatens to cut down that pluralism. Of all such developments, the most threatening has been centralization of political power. The second most threatening has been the attempt to subordinate the legislative and judicial branches of our government to the executive. This was never fully accomplished during the New Deal, but it was not for want of trying. Until 1938, the Congress was quite effectively controlled by the Executive, and there were plenty of theorists who said that this was as it should be. Entirely consistent with this line of thought was the embarrassing attempt of President Roosevelt to subjugate the Supreme Court of the United States by adding enough further members to get a majority in sympathy with his opinions.

It is only by rehearsing in detail this overriding importance of pluralism in all its manifestations as our sure bulwark against the pressure of the times toward absolutism that one can fully explain why the adherents of the New Republicanism feel so deeply about the restoration of the state-federal balance.

The instinctively sensed antipathy between centralization and individualism is also based on the familiar experience that the more local a government is, the more individuals can share in it. To the millions of people of this country, there is quite a difference in this respect between, say, a New England town meeting and a federal department.

The urgency of striking a new federal-state balance is high-lighted by the traditionally local character of the issues of the future: water, roads, power, housing, localized unem-ployment and schools. The implication is that, even in a time of peace and prosperity, with no national crisis calling for national action, these essentially local responsibilities are going to become national problems.

We are entering an era, therefore, in which the views of a political group on the proper federal-state sharing of respon-sibility are of crucial importance. If you have an Administra-tion which lapses comfortably into the habit of applying sweeping federal remedies for all ills, you may look for an-other era of concentration of power in Washington and withering-away of state governments—this time perhaps for-ever. For if Washington ultimately dominates the scene in questions of water supply, roads and streets, power, houses and education, how much does this leave of the everyday responsibilities of states and municipalities?

The need is for two things: first, there must be a clear once-and-for-all acceptance of the principle that, other things being equal, as much power and responsibility and opportun-ity for independent revenues as possible should be assigned to the states—and not the other way around. Second: new devices and mechanisms must be invented and tried, to bring federal and state and municipal resources to bear upon these looming issues. What works for the water supply problem may not work for roads or schools; but the partnership con-cept, which has been the key to the New Republican han-dling of the problem, must continue to be the underlying idea of the relationship. The states must accept the fact that these problems, and many others like them, have assumed a degree of gravity which compels the federal government to act in ways which in earlier times seemed inappropriate; the federal government, in turn, must never allow itself to follow the line of least resistance, which is simply to brush the states aside and take over, for, if it does, we shall soon see the end of the unique federal-state-local balance that has served so well to maintain the rights and the importance of individual persons.

A final reason why we instinctively abhor centralization is that we sense that it would lead to a deadening uniformity, a failure to adapt to local conditions and preferences, and a suppression of that very multiplicity which is the breeding-ground of progress. Before we deplore too loudly the bewildering profusion of differing state statutes, let us remind ourselves that it is out of just such freedom to experiment that important innovations come. If Wisconsin wants to go into the life insurance business, or North Dakota into the granary business, if Rhode Island wants to provide weekly cash benefits during sickness, or if Mississippi wants to see how it works to prohibit alcoholic beverages and simultaneously impose a tax on their sale—let them try. If the idea proves to be unsound, the country as a whole is not harmed. If the idea proves successful, it may lead the way to progress for all states. Some observers look our system over and can find no word for it but "chaotic." Be that as it may; but let us never forget the words of Henry Brooks Adams: "Chaos often breeds life, when order breeds habit."

In the last analysis, what all this is about is not the protection of the rights of one governmental entity from another governmental entity. It is the protection of the rights of the person. If we ever forget this, the whole process of decentralization is pointless. And so, when we speak of states' rights, or federal rights, we must remember that people have rights too; and it is the promotion of their rights that is the final objective of all our political institutions.

3

The Government-Business Balance

The underlying tenet of the New Republicanism in relation
to business is this: the inherent incentives, drives and energies
of private enterprise should be released and encouraged, as
the proved motive force of our economy; but at the same
time there should be just enough government activity (and
no more) to avoid extreme tendencies in the business cycle,
to protect the public against harmful practices, and to ensure
adequate protections against the human hazards of a risk
economy.

In this country, unlike many European countries, we do
not find one major party, such as the Socialists, clearly
against private enterprise, while the other major party is for
it.

Yet there is a difference between the New Republicanism
and its Opposition on this point which, while more subtle, is
of crucial importance to our future economic health.

The difference is between having faith in private enterprise, and not quite having faith in it.

It is also the difference between, on the one hand, believing, as most Americans do, that private business, big or small,
is a constructive force which brings us jobs and material
prosperity, and, on the other hand, believing that business is

something to be abused whenever it is politically convenient but never quite respected or trusted.

And it is the difference between concentrating your economic energies on building a sober, sound, solid prosperity, as against worrying about fending off a depression which is conceived to be always just round the corner under a private enterprise system.

Building Prosperity versus Fighting Depression

A showdown test separating those who have faith in private enterprise from those who do not quite have faith came in early 1954.

As the result both of sharp reductions in defense procurement and of the deflating of some excessive inventories, there was a substantial increase in unemployment in early 1954. Spokesmen for the Opposition declared that we were in danger of a depression and that the government must immediately do something grandiose to stave off this impending collapse. Under pressure of the most acute kind, including an imminent election, the Eisenhower Administration staked its future on the fundamental soundness of the private enterprise economy and on its ability to work itself out of the downturn without drastic government action.

The Administration was right, and the economy went into a steady sustained climb.

Yet even as late as the first quarter of 1955, when the Gross National Product was running at the annual rate of $375 billion, compared with $360 billion in 1954 and $364 billion in 1953, the really dedicated ultra-Fair-Deal economists persisted in proclaiming their lack of faith in the expansive power of private enterprise unassisted by special government stimulation. Dr. Leon Keyserling, Chairman of the Council of Economic Advisers during the Fair Deal, and

the accepted spokesman for this point of view, made the following comments during the hearings on President Eisenhower's 1955 Economic Report:

I think we are threatened by a long-term trend of rising chronic
unemployment. . . .
If [the economy] expands only 3 per cent, and that is an opti-
mistic forecast, I would expect the true level of unemployment
sometime within 1955 to rise by 1 to 2 million.

The level of unemployment promptly *fell* by one million.
And the economy expanded, between the 1954 rate and
the annual rate for the last quarter of 1955, not 3 per cent
but over 10 per cent.
All of which shows how far the exponents of this school
of economic thought fall short of understanding the inherent vitality of private enterprise, even when they are making
a self-announced attempt to give expression to their idea of
"optimism."
However, when we reached the point where prosperity
had to be admitted even by the most grudging, critics begin
to announce that we are prospering too much and must
surely be headed for another depression.
In short, if things are going downhill, they say you are on
your way to depression, and if things are going uphill, you
are also on your way to depression.
It reminds me of a Pogo cartoon which appeared on March
29, 1955. Churchy La Femme comes striding in feeling won-
derful and saying, "Howdy, Folks! WHAT a day! WHAT a
day! Got up early and had NO trouble eatin' breakfast most
of the morning. Next LUNCH! An' WHAT a lunch! SAME THING
as for breakfast excep' MORE. . . . Then all afternoon a-
writin' a poem. . . . No trouble with the rhymes. . . . No
trouble with the meter. Good luck been mine all day. . . ."

Then Churchy's face becomes clouded, and he exclaims, "It's enough to give a man the WHIM WHAMS."

Pogo asks: "Why Whim Whams?"

To which Churchy replies: "Man, havin' so much GOOD LUCK is a sure sign of BAD LUCK!"

Now what really happened? It has become habitual to talk about the period of business growth after the summer of 1954 as a "boom." This is somewhat misleading, if by "boom" is meant an unrestrained runaway headlong plunge in the direction of unsound expansion leading to an eventual "bust."

Certainly, almost every line on every graph showing economic growth slanted upward and broke all-time records. The Gross National Product in the last quarter of 1955 ran at the annual rate of $397 billion—far beyond the most sanguine expectations of a a few years earlier. Retail sales, power output, steel production—almost anything you care to name progressed to larger and larger volume. Total employment passed the 65 million mark; average wages in manufacturing reached almost eighty dollars a week; real take-home pay in stabilized purchasing-power was the highest ever.

Why then was this different from the old-fashioned uncontrolled boom?

One reason is that it was not accompanied by inflation. The cost of living remained stable over a three-year period.

Another is that not only the government but private businessmen as well had learned to watch this movement with unsleeping vigilance, and to apply restraints at places where unruly or unhealthy excess of activity appeared. In 1955, for example, the Federal Reserve Banks gently but firmly began to raise their rediscount rates to tighten slightly the credit supply, when the amount of credit buying began to look somewhat out of line. Stock market margins were tightened, and government terms for housing credit were stiffened a little—nothing very severe, but just enough to exert a cautionary effect and serve notice on private lenders that they might take a careful look at their own policies.

How did it come about that Opposition economists and spokesmen acquired a collective fixation upon depression? The answer is not hard to find. The Democratic Party rose to its greatest heights, and won itself a degree of popularity which kept it in office for twenty years, because of its varied and vigorous depression-fighting activities. It won the support of most leaders of organized labor; it built a reputation for humanitarianism and concern for the underprivileged; it managed to associate itself with the interests of the common man. *It did all this without bringing real prosperity.* It did it by alleviating the effects of a persistent depression which it was unable to cure (unemployment in 1939 was still 17.2 per cent) and which was cured only by war.

Now, when you have made your reputation and won your success by a certain kind of activity, naturally you cling to the formula which proved popular before. So it is only natural that those members of the Opposition whose hearts are still in the thirties continue to see depressions behind every bush, following these revelations with a set of recommendations for federal expenditures and control drawn from New Deal days.

Another reason for this depression mentality is an almost pathological preoccupation with statistics on unemployment. When every other economic indicator has been examined, and the unanimous verdict is vigorous health and growth, the inevitable voices are raised to say, "That is all very well, but you still have two and a half million unemployed; there must be something wrong and the federal government should do something about it."

The involuntary unemployment of a breadwinner with a
family is a serious tragedy—no question about that. The question is whether there will be more or less such tragedies under the competing ideas of how to build a flourishing economy. The Opposition syllogism seems to run like this:

> In the thirties, unemployment was the chief symptom
> of depression.
> There is some unemployment now.
> Therefore we now have some depression and should use
> the depression-fighting measures of the thirties.

The fallacy in this syllogism is this: the kind of unemployment we have now is different from the kind that prevailed
in the depression. That was unemployment *because* of depression; we now have some unemployment *in spite of* prosperity.

The true character of the problem is not revealed by the
one monolithic figure on national unemployment of, say, 4
per cent. We did not in 1955 have a general nation-wide
unemployment problem. In fact, there were labor shortages
in various occupations and skills, such as engineering.

The lump-sum total of unemployment includes, for a start,
hundreds of thousands of people who are merely between
jobs—the category called "frictional unemployment" by economists. There is nothing unhealthy about the existence of this
block of unemployed; in fact, if it did not exist we would
really have cause for worry, for then we would know that the
restless compulsion to self-improvement and freedom of
movement which has always characterized our labor force
had been stultified.

Another large part of the figure is accounted for by stu-
dents, housewives, young people, people living on pensions,
and others who work when they get a chance, and who de-

clare themselves unemployed when out of a job, but to whom
unemployment is not the same kind of disaster it is to a factory worker who has six children, a mortgage on his house
and several installment contracts to keep up.

Most of the remaining unemployed are the victims of
some kind of chronic local situation, such as the unemployment in the Pennsylvania and West Virginia coal fields, or in
the New England textile towns.

It was undoubtedly partly considerations of this kind which
led President Truman to say, in an exclusive interview with
Arthur Krock, that the economy could support five million
unemployed.

This kind of unemployment is definitely a serious problem,
and President Truman's level of tolerable unemployment is
much too high; but the point is that its cure is not to be
found in the sweeping panaceas for nation-wide depression
unemployment that were used in the thirties. The cure
rather lies in intensive action, of the type described later
in Chapter 5, addressed to the particular local or industrial
difficulty.

How to Have the Country Prosper

The New Republicanism believes that the way to have the
country prosper is to stop inflation, check government spending, balance the budget, encourage business venturing and
confidence, maintain and increase consumer purchasing
power, reduce government competition and interference to a
minimum, and, recognizing that there will be ups and downs
in the business cycle of even the most sound economy, maintain just the right amount of government scrutiny to avoid
excesses that damage the public interest and the well-being
of individual persons.

The years 1953 to 1956 produced something that this

country had not seen for many years: a generally high level of prosperity which was maintained without benefit of a prewar, wartime or postwar stimulation.

We are all thankful for this, but most of us have too easily taken it for granted, and have failed to note two things that are of crucial significance politically.

The first is that the accomplishment is unique in recent history. It cannot honestly be said of the New Deal or the Fair Deal.

The twenty years from 1932 to 1952 may be roughly summed up as follows, using the Opposition's own favorite measuring rod, unemployment, as the test:

From 1932 to 1941 there was peace, but no prosperity. After six years of New Deal stimulation, business was still so bad that in 1938 10.4 million people out of a work force of 54.6 million—or almost a fifth—were still unemployed. This means that the percentage of unemployment was almost six times as great as it was toward the end of 1955. By 1939, there were still 9.5 million unemployed, and by 1940, 8.1 million. Even in 1941, with the stimulus of war preparation and aid to the Allies, unemployment dropped only to 5.6 million—still almost 10 per cent, compared with 3 to 3½ per cent late in 1955.

In 1942 came the entry of this country into the war. Unemployment dropped and, of course, at the height of the war there were actual labor shortages.

In 1946, 1947 and 1948, the pent-up demands created by consumer shortages during the war gave a special impetus to business, and the annual unemployment figure remained between 3.4 and 3.9 per cent.

Then came the downturn of 1949–1950, when this war-created demand had spent itself, and unemployment went up over three million and well over 5 per cent.

The Korean conflict intervened, and unemployment averaged 3 per cent and 2.7 per cent in 1951 and 1952.

That, in brief, is the 1932–1952 story of the relation between peace and prosperity, and it tempted some uncharitable observers to suggest that perhaps this country could never after the nineteen-twenties really sustain a high-level rate of business activity apart from some kind of war-connected stimulus.

This is why the slogan "Peace and Prosperity" is more remarkable than it sounds. Peace without prosperity we have had; and prosperity without peace. But the *combination* of peace and prosperity is what distinguishes the era of New Republicanism.

The second fact that needs stress is that there is a definite relation between the policies of the Eisenhower Administration and the achievement of this economic growth.

Everyone concedes the advent of good times. The admission came belatedly from some quarters, which is understandable; a few still speak sourly of "this so-called prosperity"; but the facts are so plain that attempts to deny them have ceased.

What is important now is to note that the economic doctrines and activities of this Eisenhower Administration made this period of economic health possible.

Things like this do not just happen. It may sometimes seem that way to those who live through this kind of period. We take it in our stride, and compliment ourselves on the sturdy resiliency of good old American private enterprise—but we are apt to overlook the quiet but profoundly effective changes in policy, direction and climate for which the new Administration and new political philosophy were directly responsible.

Is the simultaneous appearance of the New Republican

Administration and good times nothing more than a charming coincidence? Or is there some kind of causal connection? By what policies and actions did the Eisenhower Administration help, specifically, to bring this about?

President Eisenhower gave a detailed answer in his 1956 Economic Report, most of which is summarized in the following passage:

First, by removing direct controls over prices and wages, which had outlived their usefulness.

Second, by preserving an actively competitive environment and assisting new and small businesses.

Third, by curtailing governmental activities that could be handled as well or better by private enterprise.

Fourth, by restricting public expenditures, and yet adding to the country's defensive strength and its stock of public assets, especially highways, hospitals, and educational facilities.

Fifth, by lightening the burden of taxes imposed on individuals and business.

Sixth, by extending the ties of trade and investment with other nations of the Free World.

Seventh, by tempering the impact of unemployment, old age, illness, and blighted neighborhoods on people, yet not impairing self-reliance.

Eighth, by extending the automatic workings of our fiscal system that tend to offset or cushion changes in income arising from changes in economic activity.

Ninth, by attacking fundamental causes of weakness in the farm situation.

Tenth, by acting promptly and resolutely when either recessionary or inflationary influences in the general economy became evident.

Let us examine some of these in more detail.

Our Most Underestimated Issue: Inflation

The late Joseph Schumpeter of Harvard in a paper read to the American Economic Association in December, 1949, said that it is inflation rather than unemployment that destroys stability in the twentieth century. Schumpeter was deeply concerned for the survival of our free society, not because of unemployment, but because American public opinion did not understand the danger of inflation.

Peter F. Drucker, in writing in the June, 1955, *Harper's Magazine,* adds this commentary:

Inflation is not only an impersonal and general danger to society —the breeder of class hatred and the destroyer of the middle class. In an economy where the great mass of people have become long-term creditors (through their insurance and pension holdings) and where as much as half of the employed population is on fixed salaries which do not readily adjust to changes in money values, *inflation may cause more individual suffering than even widespread unemployment.* This statement—obvious to any German, Frenchman, Italian, or Austrian (not to mention the people behind the Iron Curtain)—is still totally incomprehensible to most Americans. [Italics supplied]

In the perspective of history, it may well turn out that the greatest economic achievement of the Eisenhower Administration was the recognition of the true importance of safeguarding monetary stability and the taking of effective action to halt inflation, while the most damaging weakness of Fair Deal Opposition economics was its too-tolerant attitude toward an ever-increasing cost of living and a willingness to accept it as the price of expansion and full employment.

The comparative record on this score is seen in the tables on retail prices. Taking the 1947–1949 average retail price level as 100, the level of retail prices rose as follows:

1933:	55.3
1937:	61.4
1942:	69.7
1945:	76.9
1946:	83.4
1947:	95.5
1948:	102.8
1951:	111.0
1952:	113.5
1953:	114.4

By contrast, here are the figures since the advent of the Republican Administration:

1953:	114.4
1954:	114.8
1955:	114.5

What this means to wage earners can be shown by comparing growth in apparent wages under current dollars with what happens to real wages in terms of actual purchasing power.

The figure which best shows the real economic position and progress of the wage earner is "net spendable earnings," adjusted for changes in the value of the dollar. This amount is arrived at by taking gross average weekly earnings of production workers in manufacturing, subtracting deductions for income and social security taxes, and then adjusting them to the purchasing power of 1947–1949 dollars.

If you want a really dramatic demonstration of what inflation and increased taxes can do to an apparent increase in wages, look at what happened between the years 1944 and 1952, for example:

	Gross Average Weekly Earnings	Net Spendable Average Weekly Earnings Worker with No Dependents 1947–1949 dollars
1944:	$46.08	$50.92
1952:	67.97	49.04
Up	$21.89	*Down* $ 1.88

What an illusion! All during this period, while sensational increases in wages were being negotiated, and while presumably the working man was getting the impression that the Fair Deal was doing a lot for him since his wage seemed to increase almost 50 per cent, the actual truth was that his real weekly wage decreased by almost $2.00!

By contrast, see what has happened from 1953 to 1955:

	Gross Average Weekly Earnings	Net Spendable Average Weekly Earnings Worker with No Dependents 1947–1949 dollars
1953:	$71.69	$51.17
1955:	$76.52	$55.21
Up	$ 4.83	Up $ 4.04

It may be added that by December, 1955, the figure for net spendable earnings in 1947–1949 dollars had risen to $57.36. This means that there was a clear gain in purchasing power during those three years of $6.19 per week, contrasted with the clear loss in purchasing power of $1.88 during the nine-year period 1944–1952.

How easily we take this stabilization for granted! How soon we forget that we have seen with our own eyes the price of coffee go from eighteen cents to a dollar. Most of us have gone through a period in which the constant increase in prices was assumed as a matter of course. Labor union contracts covering millions of workers were revised to put in escalator clauses calling for automatic wage increases as the Consumer Price Index went up. It never seemed to occur to anyone that the Index might go down, or stand still; and when recently this miracle seemed to have happened, a large fraction of the escalator clauses were abandoned.

Although most people came to regard a forever-rising cost of living as inevitable, they hated it, dreaded it and constantly complained about it. By contrast, a considerable segment of the Opposition actually adopted inflation as an economic article of faith.

Before looking into the emerging contest between those who believe a stabilized dollar is the starting point for sound prosperity, and those who believe that a private enterprise system requires built-in inflation, let us ask two questions: Why is a steady inflationless monetary basis important to prosperity? And how does government check and control inflation?

The shortest way to find the answer to the first question is to put yourself in the place of a businessman pondering the question whether to undertake a certain venture. This decision is still the choice that makes the difference between vigor and stagnation in a private enterprise economy. When the question is too often answered, "No; what's the use, why take the chance?" slow death overtakes the body of business. When the answer is most often "Yes," there is life and growth and high employment.

The one element that can turn a possible "yes" into "no" more readily than any other is: unpredictability. Of course, the entrepreneur expects risk—that is the nature of enterprise. He is willing to undertake a lot of risks—the fickleness of public taste, the vagaries of the weather, the exigencies of competition, and the hazards of flood, strike, obsolescence and stockholder raids.

But success or failure, in the last analysis, is a matter of the calculation of the margin, which may sometimes be a rather narrow one, between costs and prices, and this calculation must be made in the going medium of exchange—money.

Now, if you cannot depend upon some stability in the value of that medium of exchange, how can you make business plans reaching out into a span of three or five or ten or more years? How could you, for example, bid on a project that might involve the purchasing of materials over several years? You might, say, write in an escalator clause, and make the buyer pay the higher costs. Very well, if the buyer will agree; but how about the buyer? He has to know his costs to plan his future too. Someone ultimately has to take the chance and be willing to absorb the unpredictable future cost—and that kind of someone is not easy to find in the business community when inflation is the order of the day.

On the other hand, think how it facilitates matters if, in launching an undertaking, you can say to yourself: I am reasonably certain that the dollar I am figuring in my calculations will be the same dollar three years from now. Supplies, taxes, prices and the value of earnings will not be erratically different. Hence, orderly plans can be laid with assurance, jobs can be created, men can be hired.

The second question about inflation is: how can a government help to keep it in check—assuming, of course, that it has the will to do so?

There is no single master dial that can be turned by the Council of Economic Advisers in the Old State Department Building which will automatically joggle the Consumer Price Index back into line when it begins to creep up. The prevention and control of inflation is an immensely complex and difficult thing, and it must not be thought that we are by now so wise that the amazing steadiness of the Price Index

of 1953 to 1955 can be guaranteed for the indefinite future.
The complexity of the matter is masked by the composite nature of the figure; actually, within the stable over-all figure,
the prices of particular commodities and services are apt to
be moving up and down quite freely. Some items, like medical costs, have moved up; some, like foods, mostly down;
and some both up and down. The objective, then, is not to
impose a deadening market-defying freeze on the natural
movement of all individual prices, but rather to keep a general healthy balance between the money supply and the
things money is spent on.

If signs of inflation appear, there are several things the
government can do, from either of two directions. It can
act to tighten the supply of money and credit; and it may
perhaps be able to facilitate a greater availability of goods
and services for money to be spent on. The former is the
more obvious and direct.

In a mild degree, 1955 saw the application of some of these
measures, when it began to appear that consumer and building credit was getting somewhat loose. The Federal Reserve Bank discount rate was gradually raised from 1½ per
cent to 2½ per cent. The terms of FHA and Veterans' Housing Loans were tightened. Margin requirements on the stock
market were raised. (Later, in April, 1956, the discount rate
went to 2¾ per cent, and in some areas 3 per cent.)

All these were gentle moves, but their effect was greater
than the direct impact on credit, since the entire lending
fraternity began to take the cue from these actions and voluntarily turn toward a more conservative course.

At the same time, the Treasury had been following a long-
term policy of converting more issues from short-term into
long-term, which in itself has the effect of contributing to
stability.

One of the most potent fiscal weapons is tax policy. This, being under Congressional control, and being particularly vulnerable to noneconomic considerations, especially in election years, is not an easy element to bring into alignment with the other fiscal measures to restrain inflation. It seems elementary that, if you are in a period of sharply climbing purchasing power which is widely distributed, and if the threat of inflation is in the air, and if business expansion and investment are moving as fast as the economy can stand, it is hardly the time to unleash a big fresh burst of purchasing power by a fat tax cut—again, assuming you are seriously interested in avoiding inflationary pressure.

Since an increase in the supply of money and credit will not bring inflation if it is balanced by a corresponding increase in things to spend money on, much of the thanks for avoidance of inflation must be given to the complex of factors which brought about the lively increase in production during 1953, 1954 and 1955. Many people cannot understand how they can read in the papers about new wage contracts giving "packages" worth fifteen or twenty cents an hour, and still not see a corresponding rise in the cost of living as the wage costs go into the cost of the product. The best explanation seems to be that the volume of production is so high, and the savings of improved technology so great, and the competition so keen, that prices generally just cannot move up as much as the increased costs might indicate. Although it is not easy to know just what the prices on automobiles are, there do not seem to have been actual increases anything like you might have expected as a result of the increase in steel wages and steel prices, coupled with the direct increases in labor costs under the 1955 automobile contracts, in spite of the fact that cars are becoming constantly bigger and more complicated. Automation, high production, dealer absorption and competition all conspire with high-volume sales to keep the price from shooting up.

What this means is that, so far as the government is concerned, we are here dealing with a circle—not a vicious circle, but the other kind. The checking of inflation, coupled with the other governmental policies making for lively business activity, leads to a high degree of business investment and expansion; this in turn leads to high volume of production and consumption, and to the cutting of costs due to installation of improved machinery; these things in turn produce a big flow of goods at reasonable cost to take up the purchasing power created by high wages and high employment, and serious inflationary pressure is minimized. It is not easy to start this beneficent circle in motion, but it would be quite easy to reverse it. A government that accepted as inevitable or even desirable a certain amount of inflation would soon find the circle becoming vicious—the prospect of inflation would begin to deter business risk; production and productivity would suffer; supply of goods would fall behind purchasing power, particularly if loose fiscal and tax policies were simultaneously followed and swelled the purchasing stream at just the wrong time; the competition of more money for less goods would bring more inflation, which would bring more constriction of risk capital and still less goods and still higher prices, and the deadly maelstrom would begin to pull us all down together.

Is there really anyone who questions the wisdom of the present course? Could anyone, witnessing the steady progress of the economy, seriously complain of restraints on inflation and call for a less stern attitude toward this danger?

The answer is that a considerable segment of the Opposition has apparently adopted an economic philosophy which would accept or even utilize inflation as means toward a super-high-speed expansion in which the only consideration is to maximize production and employment at all costs.

How did this extraordinary dogma develop?

It came about in this way. The people who do the economic thinking and speaking for a major part of the Opposition have, as we have seen, had their mental apparatus since the thirties geared to the attacking of depressions, real and imaginary. Now, the loosening of credit, the cutting of personal income taxes, the concentration on creating employment, even the use of deficit spending programs in proper circumstances, are familiar moves when business activity is sluggish and the economy's primary problem is to encourage spending. This prescription has been tendered so often and so long that its salesmen have almost forgotten it was designed for a low or falling rather than a high and rising business movement.

Now comes a period in which the most consecrated pessimist cannot deny that the economy is in excellent condition.

But, in the nature of politics, the Opposition seems to believe it must oppose. Unfortunately, some take this to mean that it must oppose on *all* policies, even the most conspicuously successful. But this raises the sticky problem: on what ground do you attack an economic policy and record that has brought material well-being beyond anything we have previously known?

The difficulty of the problem accounts for the desperateness of the answer.

The answer we are given is that even all this is not good enough. We are told we must have literally full employment. We are told we must have no dips—not even little ones—in the business cycle. We are told we must "rev up" the productive machine to a supercharged forced-draft pitch and create, through government policies and spending, a permanent boom at the absolute maximum peak of which our economy is capable.

How is this to be done? By using the same old depression-fighting gadgets: supereasy credit, loose fiscal and tax policy, and massive federal deficit spending on public works. If inflation threatens, another familiar armory of weapons is at hand: price control, wage control, materials allocation, production control and trade regulation. But, since we know from experience that these things do not really bridle inflation completely or for long, the Opposition implicitly accepts the unavoidable degree of inflation as the price that must be paid for this high-powered kind of expansion.

Symptoms of this economic philosophy turn up in the news constantly. Although at the end of 1955, unemployment was down to about 3 per cent, with most of it accounted for by the special circumstances discussed earlier, demands were constantly being made that the federal government somehow create more employment.

When Veterans Administration loan terms were modified so that closing costs could not be included in the loan, there was some outcry, even though the terms still permitted the generous privilege of financing a home with no down payment whatever. When moves were taken to tighten credit slightly, through the increase in the Federal Reserve discount rate, there was a chorus of protest, charging that the Administration was trying to depress the building boom and create unemployment.

Our economists have learned a lot from the lessons of the past on how to deal with the business cycle. They know how to apply stimulants when the business cycle is going down, through such measures as credit ease, tax relief and accelerated spending. They also know how to tighten up when things are shooting ahead too fast and threatening inflation, through such reverse moves as tighter credit, tighter tax policy and deferred spending. In other words, economists know how to apply the accelerator when things are slowing down and how to apply the brakes when things are gaining too much speed. But what no one has ever figured out is what to do when the driver is someone who insists on stepping on the gas when he ought to be applying the brakes.

How Taxes Affect Prosperity

A dramatic contrast between the economics of the New Deal and of the New Republicanism can be seen in the way the two dealt with taxes in a time of business downturn.

In the period from 1932 to 1936, unemployment was ranging between 17 and 25 per cent of the labor force. If there ever was a time when business investment needed to be encouraged and consumer spending stimulated, this was it. What happened? Terrific increases in taxes were imposed. The minimum rate of tax was raised from 1.5 per cent to 4 per cent, the maximum from 25 per cent to 79 per cent. Individual income tax exemptions were reduced from $3,500 to $2,500 for married people. A capital stock tax was enacted. Dividends were deprived of their exemption from normal tax. The corporate tax rate was raised. An undistributed profits tax was invented, which could go as high as 27 per cent. Estate taxes were boosted from a maximum of 20 per cent to 70 per cent. A gift tax of up to 52 per cent was put in. A whole array of excise taxes came along, on such items as gasoline, refrigerators, automobiles and toilet goods.

These moves, together with the well-justified expectation that taxes were going to get worse every year, not only stifled buying power of individuals and businesses; they tended to discourage investment by creating a fear of what the future might hold.

Twenty years later, in 1954, a business downswing got under way partly as the result of a necessary inventory adjustment and partly as the result of the sharp drop in military spending attending the cessation of fighting in Korea.

If the same policies which prevailed in 1934 had had their way in 1954, we might well have witnessed a series of stiff tax increases to provide the funds for a variety of government spending and make-work projects to take up the unemployment that was rapidly growing. But here is where the contrast appears.

The Eisenhower Administration took just the opposite course. It put into effect a reduction in personal income taxes averaging around 10 per cent for the lower and middle income brackets, to take effect January 1, 1954. The excess profits tax was terminated at the same time. In March, 1954, a big cut in excise taxes was put through. Then the complete overhaul of the Internal Revenue Code was passed, which straightened out many unfair features of the tax, liberalized depreciation allowances on new investment, lowered slightly the double tax on dividends, and provided tax relief in a variety of individual situations to people whose need for relief was based on some special position.

All this added up to a tax cut, on an annual basis, of 7.4 billion dollars, with about two out of every three dollars of saving going directly to individuals.

The comparative results?

By 1938, after six years of New Deal tax policy, there were still ten million unemployed—almost a fifth of the labor force—and the depression seemed to have become chronic, with no prospect of a way out.

By the last half of 1955, the very next year after the New Republican tax moves, unemployment dropped to between

2 and 2½ million, or about 3 to 3½ per cent of the labor force, and a period of genuine good times was firmly established.

There were many difficulties and mistakes besides a questionable tax policy that impeded recovery in the thirties, and there were many moves in addition to a sound and well-timed tax policy that contributed to righting the economy quickly in 1954. But the effect, both direct and psychological, of tax cuts or increases is so important that a wrong direction here could undo a lot of other efforts that might be right.

One would have thought that the lesson of the relation between tax policy and the state of the business cycle had been by now thoroughly learned by everyone. And yet one of the standard lines of attack on the Eisenhower Administration runs something like this: "Why were you cautious about recommending a tax reduction in 1956 when the budget was in balance? You did not hesitate to cut taxes in 1954, even at the expense of unbalancing the budget."

Anyone who launches this line of criticism must be implying that one of two things is wrong: either he thinks that taxes should not have been cut in 1954, in which case he convicts himself of ignorance of the elementary principle calling for tax cuts to offset business decline, or he thinks that a large tax cut should have been promised at the very beginning of 1956, in which case he convicts himself of ignorance of the danger of inflation when indiscriminate tax cuts are added to other potential inflationary pressures in a time of high and expanding demand and business activity.

There is one more important fact about taxes: they are not substantially raised or lowered merely on a whim. If they are to be cut, there must be a husbanding of resources and a tightening of government housekeeping to make the cut feasible. Conversely, when taxes are steeply raised, it is usually the concomitant of a deliberate policy of government spending.

You have to take your choice. You cannot realistically expect to indulge simultaneously in huge increases in government spending to create employment, and big cuts in taxes to create employment. This might conceivably be possible for a very brief period, but it could hardly be called a sane fiscal policy. The key to the matter is timing: to act so promptly that it would never be necessary to take such drastic dual action. When credit is eased and taxes are lowered at the first sign of a downturn in business activity, you still have your basic reservoir of purchaser and investor confidence which can be refreshed by these moves. But if the downturn has gone too far, and the reservoir of confidence is drained dry, there may be nothing left for these stimulants to act upon.

A policy of reducing taxes as a countermeasure to business recession cannot exist in a vacuum; it can exist only as part of a series of related policies, one of which must be a genuine campaign to cut government expenditures.

Cutting government expenditures is not so easy as some might have you believe. The old notion that the federal government is a sort of gigantic rabbit warren filled with paper-pushing bureaucrats most of whom have been hired in order to make their boss a bigger man is absolutely false. Where it is possible to compare the number of people for a given operation in a private business as against government, you will often find the private business using many times the personnel for the same work.

You have to live through a genuine economy drive to appreciate how thoroughgoing it must be. At the one extreme, the Defense Department cuts billions from its budget by imaginative and modern changes in the entire concept of defense and military preparedness, while actually enhancing our strength. At the other extreme, you discover one day that the yellow pad you get from the supply room contains coarser paper, that your new letterheads are printed instead of embossed, and that your department is being held accountable to pay postage on every letter it sends out instead of having a free franking privilege.

Through economies of these kinds, large and small, military and nonmilitary, the Eisenhower Administration promptly cut federal expenditures nine billion dollars in eighteen months.

The tax policy could not have existed without the economy policy. That is why a political philosophy must have a consistent over-all pattern, for each part supports the other, and in many instances one part is not possible without the other.

How Much Government Control?

Everyone by now admits that there must be some government regulation of business.

The question is: how much?

The answer of the New Republicanism and of the American Consensus is: enough to protect the public interest, the rights of people and the integrity and health of the private enterprise system, and no more.

In practically every case of government regulation that still survives, you will find that there is a specific evil being avoided which no one other than the federal government could be expected to deal with. At the same time, the government does not get into the main stream of business and attempt to control the vital variables which make the difference between success and failure, or profit and loss—such as prices, volume, product, markets, wages, labor contracts or materials.

For example, the Securities and Exchange Commission enforces rules to prevent the stock exchanges from being rigged or deceptive, to forestall cheating by corporate insiders by use of inside information, to block the misleading of stockholders through false proxy statements, and to ensure that full information is available to investors in connection with new securities issues. But it does not tell you what stocks you can buy or sell, or even express an opinion on whether they are sound or not. If a registration statement for a new security is completely true, and if the truth so stated shows that the security is no good and that the promoters are getting away with murder, the federal law at least is satisfied. The rules make sure that the stock markets fairly reflect the results of free trading, but if free trading fairly leads to severe hardships for some, the SEC has no jurisdiction over that.

Much government regulation is necessitated by the kind of natural monopoly involved, just as local government regulation of monopolies like streetcars or electric service is taken for granted. There are only a limited number of television and radio channels; someone has to parcel them out and see that the licensees do not abuse the public interest while in possession of this monopoly of a channel. Only the federal government could do this kind of job—hence we must have a Federal Communications Commission. In a somewhat similar sense, there must be public review of use of airlanes, rail lines and waterways. And so no one now questions having an Interstate Commerce Commission, or a Civil Aeronautics Authority and Board, or a Federal Power Commission.

Again, our everyday safety and health in a complex world require that someone constantly enforce standards that we cannot individually enforce ourselves. How could we live in this fast-moving era if we could not assume that the contents of the can of beans we buy are not poisonous, that the plane we ride in has been properly inspected, and that the shampoo we apply will not burn our hair off? Thus it happens that we have the Federal Trade Commission, the Food and Drug Laws, the many safety controls in transportation and the rules against false advertising.

To draw an example from an entirely different field: back in the last century we decided once and for all that we were not going to let free enterprise be run into the ground by monopolies and restraints of trade. And so antitrust activities are constantly and vigilantly carried on by the Department of Justice and the Federal Trade Commission, not as an interference with the principle of freedom of enterprise, but as a protection of that principle. (Fifty-two antitrust actions were commenced between September 30, 1954, and September 30, 1955—almost 50 per cent more than in the last similar period before the Republican Administration assumed office.)

These examples are cited from among the dozens that could be mentioned to make one simple point: government "control" or regulation of these kinds is a help rather than a hindrance to free business. What would happen to retail trade in packaged foods or cosmetics or drugs if people could not buy and use them with confidence born of government regulation? What would happen to the securities business if investors could not rely on the truth of a prospectus? What kind of television business could flourish if the air were saturated by broadcasters all trying to use the available channels on an every-man-for-himself basis? Who would patronize a commercial airline if there were no way of knowing that the lines were reputable and safe, no investigations of causes of accidents and no ordering of traffic?

It is time, then, to break whatever is left of the habit of

thought which mentally pictures government regulation as somehow antagonistic to business. Sometimes it is not only beneficial, but indeed indispensable to the success of the businesses affected.

At the other extreme there are some kinds of government interference with business that are both unnecessary and harmful.

This is almost always the case when the regulation attempts to take the normal processes of the market or of bargaining out of the hands of the parties. We tolerate price and wage and materials controls in wartime, just as we tolerate a lot of other interferences with our normal liberties. But the great majority of Americans have never become so inured to these measures as to accept them as part of our normal life apart from severe emergencies.

Starting only thirteen days after he took office, President Eisenhower gave expression to this American Consensus by putting an end to a whole array of price, wage and other controls, at a time when his Opposition was asserting that this could only lead to disaster.

The inflationist cult of economics, which was described a little earlier, almost necessarily accepts price, wage and materials controls as devices which must be kept, if not always active, at least always at the ready. A person who believes that an inflation of a few per cent per year is a desirable driving force to keep the economy booming will also believe that, when necessary to curb such an inflation, price and other controls should be constantly available.

But one who believes that the economy can and will flourish without inflation if given a decent chance will, as President Eisenhower did, remove artificial controls in the full confidence that the inner health of the economy will assert itself.

This is not to say that there are to be absolutely no limits on free bargaining. You cannot freely bargain yourself into a monopoly. You cannot freely bargain to sell short the stock of a corporation you control. And you cannot freely bargain, in most industries, to pay a wage which is so sub-substandard as to be degrading to the worker and to create potential personal and community problems.

Accordingly, you find the Eisenhower Administration vigorously enforcing antitrust and SEC laws, and obtaining an increase in the minimum wage.

Freedom to bargain, then, covers almost the entire range of business and employment relations, but, when certain human or public or safety or ethical interests are threatened, the law draws a line and says, "Below this you may not go." There is nothing in this inconsistent with the basic idea of freedom of contract, any more than there is a violation of personal freedom when one is forbidden to carry on rifle practice at the corner of Pennsylvania Avenue and Fourteenth Street.

The Business of Government

The business of government is government, not business.

Of all the activities of government *vis-à-vis* business, the one which combines all the most hurtful and inexcusable features is the direct operation of business ventures in competition with private entrepreneurs.

Some of the hundred or so business ventures which the Eisenhower Administration found the government involved in were: railroad and ship operation, scrap metal baling, hotel operation, furniture repair, baking, sawmilling, ropemaking, laundries and dry cleaning, tire retreading, life insurance, motion pictures, and the manufacture of clothing, paint and ice cream.

It is a difficult and time-consuming matter to conduct an orderly liquidation of such of these ventures as ought to be returned to private firms. But the objective of the New Republicanism is clear—and it certainly conforms to the feelings of most Americans: the government should get out of such businesses as are the normal domain of private enterprise.

Some progress has been made. The Defense Department has made an inventory of commercial services and operations, and the Hoover Commission has made a study with recommendations, while the Commerce Department has been continuously engaged in looking for competitive activities among government agencies. All this has laid the necessary groundwork for a systematic reduction of inappropriate commercial projects. Quite a few have actually been disposed of: the Inland Waterways Corporation, for $9,000,000; the Bluebeard's Castle Hotel in the Virgin Islands for $410,000; various tin and rubber plants; a uniform factory; some paint-manufacturing facilities; coffee-roasting operations; sawmills; and map-making activities.

The effect of getting the government out of business is not merely to remove the impropriety of placing government in competition with private venturers in a private enterprise system; there are also outright gains to the government, not only in the sale price, but in the federal, state and local taxes collected.) The amounts involved are considerable. For example, in disposing of twenty-five synthetic rubber plants for $272 million, the government showed a profit of $158 million over the depreciated book value of the plants. There may also be savings to the taxpayer in getting out of a loss operation, as in the case of the Inland Waterways Corporation, which over a period of years had lost more than fifteen million dollars of the taxpayer's money.

In all this, however, caution should be exercised not to go overboard in pursuit of a salutary principle. When someone suggests that a government department which has to do mimeographing work in the course of its duties should fire its staff mimeographer and send for a commercial mimeographer whenever a job has to be done, it is time to pull up for a moment and remind ourselves what we are really getting at. Whenever, in the interests of efficiency and convenient operation, it would be normal for a private office to get certain jobs done through direct employees, it is no less justifiable for the government to do the same. The test is not whether the function could conceivably be performed under contract by an independent business agency; the test is whether it would normally be so performed in a comparable undertaking. The decision, in everyday business, whether to accomplish a given result by engaging employees as against independent contractors is a familiar one. Some stores hire their own truck drivers; some contract with United Parcel Service. Some plants hire employees to wash their windows; some contract the job to a window-washing firm.

However, the federal government still has enough business enterprises on its hands that are unjustifiable under any standard to keep it busy with the liquidation process for some time. The important thing is not whether the job is done overnight; it is rather whether the Administration in power sincerely believes the job should be done and moves as rapidly as it can to achieve it.

There is one other simple test of the propriety of federal business-type activity.

If a particular job has to be done, in the public interest, and private enterprise cannot do it, then by default it is proper for the federal government to act.

Let us try this out on what is by all odds the most explosive of all issues in this category: hydroelectric dams and power developments.

In a given case, you ask first: does this job have to be done? Let us assume the answer is yes, because of the need for flood control, improved navigation, water supply and probably irrigation and power as well.

The second question is: can private enterprise do it? Frequently the answer is no. This may be because a major part of the investment in the dam is attributable to public purposes like flood control or navigation. It may also be because the dam system may involve several states. And it sometimes is because the sheer size of the project is beyond the reach of any private entrepreneur or group.

But, once you have the dams in place, and the job is done that only the federal government could do, the inquiry enters a second phase. Is there some part of the job that can be handled from that point on as well by private enterprise as by the federal government—say, the distribution of power? If the answer is yes, the fundamental reason for federal activity disappears, and you return to your beginning assumption that, other things being equal, private enterprise should be allowed to handle everything of a commercial nature that it can.

There is no intention here to become embroiled in any specific controversy over any specific dam or power proposal, or to say that this big dam here would be better than several little dams there, or that A rather than B should build and operate a steam plant. The only purpose here is to ask whether we might not at least achieve agreement on the elementary principle stated above, recognizing that there will always be hard and close decisions on the question whether under a given set of facts the federal government is indeed the only one who can "swing the deal," and whether in a given case of power distribution "other things are equal" and greater private participation is warranted.

One gets the impression that much of the present bitter dispute about power policy is not of this latter kind of legitimate difference about the facts. It is rather the product of a far-reaching clash in political philosophies touching the all-important issue of the role of government in business.

Apparently there are those who sincerely believe that, other things being equal, the government should get in and stay in the power business. They justify this by such arguments as the fact that water power is a public resource belonging to all the people which should not be exploited for private gain. They may or may not, depending on the circumstances and locale of the statement, also argue that public power results in cheaper rates for electricity.

If those who attack the Administration's power policies are really starting from this pro-public-power-for-its-own-sake premise, and will plainly admit that this is the case, then at least we shall know in what arena to carry on the combat.

The issue is complicated by the fact that such developments as TVA involved much more than mere flood control, navigability and power. That undertaking was conceived as a sort of renaissance for an entire area. It had a pronounced social flavor, which anyone can still observe who travels through the region. The standard of living, of education and of culture of the residents of the Tennessee hills was to be raised, and was indeed raised; handicrafts were revived, and the tourist can buy pottery and hand-woven products and woodwork at the shop at Norris Dam as evidence of this cultural activity. The town of Norris itself was made a model of tidiness and planning. The landscaping and road planning and recreational facilities and all the rest are a constant joy, and can be held up to shame the unplanned towns and handi-craft-less regions which have not had the benefit of a TVA.

Yet if we attempt to settle crucial questions about public power by allowing ourselves to be unconsciously influenced by pretty pottery, we are apt to go wrong.

Maybe the federal government sometimes does have better taste than private business; maybe sometimes it does do a job more cheaply. You could argue about that for hours, since there is no agreed system of accountancy for comparing government and private costs, just as there is no agreed system of accountancy for comparing tastes in things cultural.

If you believe in the principle that the government should generally stay out of private commerce, you believe it because you know that it is the principle of private enterprise that has brought us our outstanding material well-being. In the words of President Eisenhower's 1956 State of the Union Message:

> Our competitive enterprise system depends on the energy of free human beings, limited by prudent restraints in law, using free markets to plan, organize, and distribute production, and spurred by the prospect of reward for successful effort. . . . Against the record of all other economic systems devised through the ages, this competitive system has proved the most creative user of human skills in the development of physical resources, and the richest rewarder of human effort.

If you agree with this—and the vast majority of Americans do—you do not abandon your principle whenever someone assumes to prove to you, by some system of accounting, that in a specific case the government can "get it for you cheaper."

Which is better—to have one central planner doing your planning, or to have ten million entrepreneurs each exercising his ingenuity to the full?

Which will produce the greater drive—one central government trying to supply incentives, or ten million entrepreneurs each out to make his fortune and win in the competitive race?

Which will bring out the greater ingenuity and service and inventiveness—a centralized government, or eighty million employers and employees each applying his skill and intelligence to the improvement of products and processes and services because he knows such skill and intelligence will be abundantly rewarded?

Which will elicit those daring innovations and trial-and-error decisions without which we should lapse into stagnation—a single central decision-making authority, or ten million centers of decision, any one of which can risk a wrong decision without disaster to all the rest?

To return to the initial theme of this chapter: either you believe—for reasons like these and others—in the essential rightness of free private enterprise, or you do not fully believe in it.

The New Republicanism does; and it is this clear belief which enables it to steer a straight course in the midst of stormy controversies waged on the borderline between private enterprise and limited or localized nationalization of business.

It would be helpful if an equally clear statement of principle were forthcoming from the spokesmen for the Opposition. Exactly when, and on what theory, should the government interfere with or compete with private business? We have never been told.

Is Business Good or Bad?

In about 1935, Franklin D. Roosevelt began to take an antibusiness tone which, in some degree, has characterized the utterances of many Democratic spokesmen ever since.

In fairness to President Roosevelt, it should be said that some businessmen were outspokenly anti-Roosevelt before Mr. Roosevelt was antibusinessmen. The abuse heaped upon Mr. Roosevelt in the early years of his Administration undoubtedly had something to do with his decision to fight back on a personal basis.

Be that as it may, and quite apart from the question of who started the fight, the important fact is that an atmosphere of government-business hostility was created which undoubtedly played a part in preventing any final economic recovery during Mr. Roosevelt's peacetime years. One could hardly expect the objects of such epithets as "money-changers" and "economic royalists" to undertake with much assurance the kind of extra risk investment in the future which the times required. Government-business partnership of the vigorous and effective kind which would have been necessary to pull the country out of its long slump could not exist when one of the necessary "partners" announced that "the forces of selfishness and of lust for power . . . met their master."

There will undoubtedly be those who, relying on the frailty of human memory and the tenderizing effect of time on old antagonisms, will tell us that these Democratic Administrations were never really antibusiness at heart. An attitude or atmosphere is a subjective thing; it is not easy to prove factually. But most people who lived through this period do not have to have it proved.

However, for contemporary purposes, the important question is whether the Opposition is still antibusiness in this new era.

Mr. Adlai Stevenson in October, 1955, wrote an article in *Fortune Magazine* which must be some kind of a milestone in the history of the Democratic Party. It is called "My Faith in Democratic Capitalism," and its general purpose is to call for an end of hostilities between the Democratic Party and business. He says quite candidly that Roosevelt never should have used such hard names as "economic royalists" about businessmen, but he balances this by saying that business- men themselves were not without fault when they rashly threw about such epithets as "creeping socialism." This sort of symmetrical or antiphonal theme runs through the whole article; there has been fault and lack of understanding on both sides; let's get the two great forces of our society— private enterprise and government—pulling together, and then we shall really go places.

The very partnership he is calling for in the future is al- ready an accomplished fact. It is elementary in the New Republican economic doctrine, and is one of the principal reasons for the current satisfactory state of business affairs.

All of which suggests an unavoidable question:

Who Is Joining Whom?

We have now and then heard it said that the New Re- publicans have taken over a number of items from the New Deal.

It is time we realized, however, that a few Democratic spokesmen would like to start a movement from the other side. We are witnessing, and will continue to witness, a studied attempt on the part of an occasional Democratic candidate to appropriate to himself the popular Eisenhower program and Center position. Nothing succeeds like success. The New Republican policies have ushered in an era of good feeling and good times. Their leader as a result enjoys almost universal esteem and affection. Hence, it is only sensible to become identified with as much of the successful formula as possible.

Another recent example of the Democratic inclination to make a virtue of moderation and conservatism is Dean Acheson's book, *A Democrat Looks at His Party*. Its theme is that the Democratic Party combines empiricism and conservatism. "American labor is now known throughout the world for its conservatism." "Southern conservatism is an invaluable asset." "We see now how basically conservative the Tennessee Valley Authority, for instance, was and is." "The effect of the combination of conservatism and empiricism of which I have spoken is nowhere better shown than in the actions taken by the New Deal of President Roosevelt to meet the great depression."

There was an old music-hall gag during the depression which went like this: " 'Go after business' sounds like good advice, until you remember where business has gone."

The situation is now reversed. "Business" is respected, and is given its share of credit for our high standard of living. Accordingly, it has begun to appear to some Democratic spokesmen that it would be strategically advisable to "go after business" by living down their party's antibusiness past and trying to hold forth to the world the kind of balanced attitude toward business that has been the hallmark of the New Republicanism.

The Big Business Fable

However, old habits die hard, and the demagogic value of the kind of attacks on business that have been going on for decades cannot be dispensed with entirely.

The solution of this dilemma takes a familiar form. The attack is concentrated, not on business as such, but on "Big Business."

To the extent that this sort of distinction between big and small business is a legitimate attempt to combat monopolies that violate the Sherman Anti-Trust Act, there can be no quarrel. This Administration has been as vigorous in genuine antitrust activity as any. But this broadside attack on Big Business is no such thing. The assault is entirely an emotional and political one.

We have here to do with a first-class paradox. The attack on Big Business is often done in the name of advancing the interests of labor. Yet it is in Big Business establishments that labor has attained its most prized gains. In a typical Big Business employment, the employee probably has:

—State workmen's compensation.
—Supplementary workmen's compensation by contract.
—State unemployment insurance.
—Supplementary unemployment benefits by contract.
—Federal old-age and survivors' insurance.
—Supplementary old-age pension by contract.
—Group life insurance by contract.
—A health and welfare plan, by contract.
—Cash weekly benefits for temporary nonoccupational sickness or disability.
—Medical and hospital payments, by contract.
—A whole array of fringe benefits, including paid holidays, recreational programs, etc.

Next door to this Big Business plant, where all these splendid benefits are available, there may be a little shop employing three men. The chances are that these three men will be entitled, in a typical state, to the following:
—Old-age and survivors' insurance.
And nothing else.

The Big Business plants are usually organized. It is in small business that you find the bulk of unorganized workers.

How then are we supposed to conclude from this that the big fellow is the working man's natural enemy?

The idea of disguising the inherent antibusiness attitude in the form of attack on "bigness" in business as such will not bear examination. If you offered to give a critic of Big Business *carte blanche* to do with Big Business as he pleased, he could not tell you what he would do. He is just against it, that is all.

Let us test this Big Business line of attack by examining in careful detail a favorite example used in this attack.

In 1954, the 83rd Congress, under Republican control, had before it a tax measure that, for the first time in history, was designed to rationalize the entire income tax statute from beginning to end, eliminating unfairness, plugging loopholes and adjusting relationships between the parts.

The distinctive thing about this tax bill was the amount of trouble it went to in order to give individualized relief in a variety of situations affecting the everyday problems of individuals. Instead of consuming the entire available tax reduction in an across-the-board kind of cut, it applied a considerable amount of the reduction to help out people with special personal needs.

For example, it considered the hardship experienced by families who are trying to bring up children and give them an education. It allowed all children eighteen and under to be claimed as dependents regardless of earnings, thus putting an end to the exasperating situation in which children's earnings were sometimes deliberately kept beneath the allowable limit to avoid losing their tax dependency status. The act also permitted a child to be claimed as a dependent, even if over eighteen, if he was attending school or college or receiving training on the farm. Here again, a realistic rule, recognizing the facts of family life, was substituted for an arbitrary one.

Another helpful move was the allowance of a 20 per cent tax credit on retirement income for persons who have retired, up to twelve hundred dollars. This was a "break" for retired people who, even under liberalized pension systems, still have a hard time making ends meet.

Widows and widowers with children or other single close dependent relatives were also given special attention, through an extension to them of the split income privilege.

People suffering from high medical expense also were thought of, and the medical expense deduction requirement was lowered from 5 per cent to 3 per cent.

Widows, widowers, and mothers who have to work, and who have to hire baby-sitters or other child care, at last had some special thought given to their problem, and a deduction was introduced for this kind of expense. After all, the cost of child care is, in a sense, a "business expense" to the person who has to pay for this kind of care as a condition of being able to go to work.

Farmers were given a liberalized allowance in connection with soil conservation expense.

One could go on with this kind of catalogue of carefully-thought-out adjustments to meet human problems—increased charitable deductions, more allowance for interest on credit purchases, more savings on taxation of pensions and annuities—but the principal point to be made here is merely that this tax bill was notable for the care with which it tried to meet typical human needs on a personalized basis.

Yet, from the moment it was passed, this tax act was under violent assault from some critics as a sellout to Big Business. This particular issue makes a good test case under which to examine just how much substance there really is in one of these typical Big Business attacks. For this reason, it will be well worth while to undertake a step-by-step analysis of the real merits of the controversy surrounding the action taken by this bill on taxation of corporate dividends.

One of the features of the income tax that for many years had bothered economists and tax experts was the double taxation of dividends.

This double taxation, introduced early in the New Deal, comes about because the same earnings are taxed, first, as income to the corporation, and again, as income to the stockholder when received in the form of dividends.

This double tax does not apply to business profits as such; it applies only if the business organization has the features of a corporation. It does not apply to partnerships. It does not apply to joint ventures. It does not apply to sole traders.

For example, let us suppose that there are a corporation and a partnership operating in the shoe store business side by side. The corporation (like thousands of small corporations) is owned equally by two men, Corcoran and Corby, and the partnership is also owned equally by two men, Parmenter and Parker. Each of the four men is personally fortunate enough to have to pay an average 60 per cent tax on his personal income. Suppose the corporation and the partnership each have a taxable income for the year of $100,000. What happens?

The partners in the partnership, Parmenter and Parker, are simply taxed at the average rate of 60 per cent on the $50,000 share of each. This trims off $30,000 each, and leaves each $20,000.

But in the corporation, the first thing that happens is that the corporate tax is applied to the corporation's income as such. This lops off about $46,500 for a start; $53,500 is all that is left to be distributed as a dividend. Suppose it is all distributed. Corcoran gets $26,750 and Corby gets $26,750.

But now Corcoran and Corby must each pay a 60 per cent tax on his dividend as personal income. So each pays a further tax of $16,050. This leaves Corcoran with $10,700 and Corby $10,700, compared with $20,000 for Parmenter and $20,000 for Parker, who were in the same business, made the same profits, and were in the same personal income tax bracket.

(You may ask: why does anyone use the corporate form who could possibly operate as a partnership? The answer is beyond the scope of this discussion, but often the reason is sheer habit, or convenience, or the desire for limited liability; it is true, however, that the tax discrimination has caused a considerable movement toward partnerships and away from corporations in appropriate cases.)

One can get used to almost anything, and in this country we have already become quite accustomed to this extraordinary piece of tax discrimination, although by any familiar standard it would certainly strike the impartial observer as very odd.

There is a parallel discrimination resulting from the same double tax, which has much graver consequences for the future vitality of our investment pattern. This is the distinction between the treatment of dividends on stock and interest on bonds.

To the ordinary man, stocks and bonds are roughly in the same category; they are pieces of paper, often traded on the exchanges, which entitle you, first, to some income payments from time to time, and second, to be paid some capital value when redeemed or sold. In legal theory, however, they are as different as lender and borrower. The stockholders are on the inside, owning the business and (in their corporate capacity) owing its debts. The bondholders are on the outside, acting as money-lenders to the corporation.

Taxwise, this produces a dramatic difference. The corporation can deduct from gross income the amount it pays out as interest on its bonds. It cannot do this with the dividends paid on its stock. An example will show the difference.

The Bonstok Corporation has $10,000,000 in securities outstanding, of which $6,000,000 are bonds and $4,000,000 stocks.

The Nohbon Corporation has $10,000,000 outstanding, all in stocks.

Assume both are in the same business, and have the same number of stockholders and are in every other way identical.

Each corporation makes $500,000 in the year, which it proceeds to distribute. We will suppose the bonds call for 5 per cent interest; the Bonstok Corporation therefore distributes $300,000 to its bondholders and the remaining $200,000 to its stockholders. The Nohbon Corporation distributes the entire $500,000 to its stockholders as a dividend.

When the Bonstok Corporation comes to calculate its income tax, it will immediately deduct from its gross profits the sum of $300,000 which it paid its bondholders as interest, since interest is a cost of doing business. The corporation's income tax would therefore be applied only to the remaining $200,000, and would be something like $98,500. The Nohbon Corporation could make no such deduction, but must declare the entire $500,000 as taxable income, and pay about a $254,500 tax on it at that point, as against $98,500 for the Bonstok Corporation.

It does not take a financial genius to figure out that this kind of tax system is soon going to drive as much financing as possible into the form of bonds.

Here again, there are practical and legal limits to how far the process of switching to bonds can go.

But the real danger here is not so much one of unfairness as one of possible damage to the process of risk investment in this country. Economists for some time have been concerned about the tendency of more and more capital to go into bonds and other conservative financing. There are other influences besides this tax discrimination pushing in the same direction. Notable among these is the accumulation of many billions of reserves in private company pension funds, in great insurance companies and in trust companies. For various legal and other reasons, the investments of these institutions, even when they buy equity shares, are on the conservative side; they tend to shy away from the kind of risk investment in common stocks that is the lifeblood of a progressive economy.

When, on top of this force driving money away from real venture capital, you place a tremendous tax reward upon obtaining working capital in the form of bonds rather than common stocks, you have constructed severe odds against the liberal investment of our available funds in risk capital.

Do you hear complaints that it is hard to finance a small business—hard to get backing for an exciting new invention? Remember then it is the *small* businessman, the *new* businessman, the *young* inventor, the ambitious worker wanting to go into business for himself who need risk capital obtained through common stocks and who cannot get lent capital in the form of bonds, because the latter requires security. Big Business can get loans, or get its capital from withheld earnings. It is the small, growing business that withers and dies when venture capital dries up.

The man, then, who attacks policies aimed at releasing more venture capital is attacking, not Big Business, but small business.

Now, to pick up the political story, in 1954 the Eisenhower Administration proposed to make a start in the direction of, first, correcting the discrimination against earnings in the form of dividends, and, second, removing one of the forces driving investment away from stocks and into bonds.

As a part of this over-all pattern of tax reduction, the Administration re-examined the double dividend tax. It did not propose to eliminate it. It did not even propose to cut it in half.

It merely proposed that, on his personal income tax, the stockholder could credit *4 per cent* of the amount of his dividend income. For the special benefit of small stockholders, of whom there are millions, it was further provided that the first fifty dollars of dividend should be entirely exempt from personal income tax.

This proposal brought forth the most intemperate, enraged, agonized outcry of protest that the Opposition could produce. The air was filled with cries that the Republicans had proved beyond all doubt that they were the tools of Wall Street, that the whole tax reduction was a fraud because it was all probusiness, and so on and on and on.

How much did it amount to in dollars? Out of total tax relief, beginning January 1, 1954, of *$7,400 million*, this dividend feature amounted to an estimated $204 million. *This is only 2¾ per cent of the total tax saving.*

The very ferocity of this attack on a mild, sober, scientific attempt to rectify a serious investment trend, and, at the same time, to modify slightly the discrimination between stockholders on the one hand, and partners or bondholders on the other, is the clearest evidence that there lies beneath the surface a real vein of antibusiness sentiment in the Opposition, which shows through at times like this. This has nothing to do with any distinction between Big Business and small business. There are literally hundreds of thousands of small corporations in this country, and, as shown above, it is these small corporations who most need the stimulus to investment in stocks that this change aims to provide.

Nor it is true that hitting at dividend recipients is identical with soaking the rich. Among present stockholders are 2,130,000 housewives, 20,000 members of the armed forces, 210,000 semiskilled workers, 10,000 unskilled workers, 410,000 foremen, 320,000 farmers, 590,000 clerical workers, 250,000 small merchants and 200,000 salesmen.

American families want to invest in stock if they can, and would probably do so on a greater scale if there were less tax discrimination. Now that the first fifty dollars of dividend income is completely tax-exempt, a thousand dollars or so in stock will be a very attractive investment for the man with some savings.

The vicious assaults on this dividend-tax move cannot be explained on any economic or technical basis. No attempt was made to discuss on the merits the problem of increased stagnation of venture capital, nor the problem of dividends versus interest or partnerships versus corporations. The onslaught was entirely emotional, and based on class distinctions, poor versus rich, toiler versus capitalist.

Perhaps we shall presently be asked to excuse this also as one of those little excesses of the more overwrought critics who must not be taken too literally. Mr. Stevenson has assured us in the pages of *Fortune Magazine* that the Democratic Party would like to be counted on the side of capitalism and free enterprise. This being so, should it really be thought scandalous to suggest that those whose risked savings are the backbone of our country's enterprise and new ventures should pay perhaps slightly less than double the taxes paid by secured bondholders and lenders and partners and sole traders?

Are corporations as such so evil, and stockholders as such so greedy and parasitic, that any penalty on their earnings even slightly less than double taxation must be viewed as a mortal violation of high ethical principle?

This factual inquiry into the double-dividend-tax matter has been carried on at this length because it is only in concrete situations like this that one can reliably appraise the real attitude of the Opposition toward private enterprise. After all, Opposition spokesmen nowadays are not going to rise up and cry: down with private enterprise! But they give themselves completely away by the bitterness of their fight when something like the dividend tax is at stake.

The "Big Business" line of attack sometimes manifests itself in the form of an attempt to assert that, in spite of general prosperity, small business is having a bad time. This is usually managed by selecting some isolated statistic out of context, such as the number of business failures, and trying to weave a tragic story around that figure. Let us look at the complete story, as evidenced by a number of indicators.

During the third quarter of 1955, small corporations (defined as those with under $1 million in assets) reported earnings before taxes of $446 million—an increase of more than $100 million over the $341 million they earned during the third quarter of 1954. Net sales of $18,123 million for the second and third quarters of 1955 were up $1,310 million over the corresponding quarters of 1954.

The total number of incorporations in 1955 was 139,639, an increase of about one-fifth over the 117,164 incorporations in 1954. As to business failures, the trend was downward during most of 1954, and slightly lower in 1955. Naturally the figure on failures must be looked at side by side with the figure on creation of new businesses, to have any real meaning.

The point made in the last few pages—that the 1954 tax revision would particularly help small business get equity capital—appears to be borne out by the securities market. In 1955, issues of stock between $100,000 and $300,000 totaled $269,000,000, compared with $195,000,000 for small issues in 1954—an increase of 38 per cent as against less than 10 per cent for securities generally.

Finally, in the way of statistics, it is sometimes alleged that the relative share of small business in defense procurement has been cut. This is not borne out by recent figures. Awards to small business firms during the first six months of fiscal 1956 were $1,414 million, compared with $1,268 million in the corresponding period in fiscal 1955. This represents an increase in the percentage of contract awards to small business from 15.7 per cent to 17.6 per cent.

In an age of swiftly advancing technology and high capital requirements, however, constant vigilance is necessary to see that small business is not disadvantaged. Far from neglecting small business, the Eisenhower Administration has set in motion a whole series of moves to help it.

The operations of the Small Business Administration, whose entire job is to aid small business, are being made more effective. For example, the maximum size of the loans it can make was raised in 1955. Its program also calls for a stepping-up of education of small business in opportunities for tapping the securities markets. In line with this is the corresponding proposal to simplify and modify burdensome requirements in connection with securities issues. New plans and procedures are being worked out to channel more loans of very small size to very small businesses, such as retailers and wholesalers. New relationships with development credit corporations, local and state, established for making joint loans, are part of the program.

Increased efforts are being made to ensure that a fair proportion of defense contracts and subcontracts go to small business. Thus, the Department of Defense has issued a directive requiring reports from each of its prime contractors every six months on the amount and source of subcontracts under each contract for one million dollars or more, so that a really close watch can be kept on subcontracting trends and practices. It has also directed increased set-asides for small business concerns.

Under legislation proposed by the Administration, a large increase in the activities of the Department of Commerce providing assistance on technical, managerial and marketing matters is called for. This particularly helps small business, since Big Business can hire its own technical and financial experts. The proposed Administration program for assistance to labor surplus areas would also tend very heavily in the direction of helping small business.

One of the surest proving-grounds of an Administration's attitude on Big Business and small business is its antitrust policy, record and proposals. Nothing could be more out of character for a supposed Big Business administration than for it to be found redoubling antitrust activities.

In 1955 the number of proceedings brought against corporate mergers was greater than in all previous years since 1950, when the antimerger amendment to the Clayton Act was passed.

New orders prohibiting price discriminations hurtful to small competitors were issued.

New orders against exclusive dealing opened new distribution opportunities and outlets to smaller manufacturers previously closed by dominant competitors.

Many legal actions against price-fixing and market-sharing

were carried through, as well as suits dissolving group boycotts.

In addition, a full-scale job of re-examining the antitrust laws to improve and strengthen them has been undertaken. This began with a thorough investigation by a National Committee to Study the Antitrust Laws. Two of its recommendations have already become law. One raises maximum penalties under the Sherman Act from five thousand dollars to fifty thousand dollars. The other gives the federal government the right to sue for the damages it suffers as a result of antitrust violations.

President Eisenhower's 1956 program for more effective antitrust and antimerger action includes a number of new items:

—A requirement of advance notice to the antitrust authorities when firms in interstate commerce other than small firms plan to merge.
—Federal regulation of banking mergers.
—Requirement of federal approval for acquisition of banks by holding companies.
—Clear authorization of the federal government to act in merger transactions when either party is engaged in interstate commerce.
—Finality of Federal Trade Commission cease-and-desist orders unless appealed.
—Authorization of the Attorney General in civil cases to compel production of documents without going to a grand jury.

These, and other improvements that have flowed and will flow from the National Committee's findings, added to the impressive record of volume and variety of actions to pre-

serve free competition, should suffice to show that the New
Republicanism is effectively carrying out the American Consensus, which insists upon the maintenance of healthy competitive markets and detests monopoly.

The Opposition has tried hard to characterize the Eisenhower Administration as a Business Administration. It has
found that it cannot do so by reference to what the Administration has actually done, since the Eisenhower program is a
matter of record, and that program, as a reader of this
book can easily see, is a well-rounded one benefiting all
our people generally and singling no group out for special
privileges.

Frustrated in this line of attack, the Opposition has tried to
make its point by resort to personalities. It has attempted to
create the impression that the key people in the Administration are all big businessmen. It is about time the facts on this
point were put clearly on the record.

Here are the backgrounds of the men who will typically
be found around the Cabinet table:

The President: a general and university president.

The Vice President (Nixon): a former member of Congress.

The Assistant to the President (Sherman Adams): a former
Governor and Congressman.

The Secretary of State (Dulles): a lawyer.

The Secretary of Defense (Wilson): engineer and businessman.

The Secretary of the Treasury (Humphrey): lawyer and
businessman.

Attorney General (Brownell): a practicing lawyer.

Secretary of Commerce (Weeks): former Senator and
businessman.

Secretary of Agriculture (Benson): farmer, marketing specialist in a University Extension Service, and secretary of a Co-op.

Postmaster General (Summerfield): businessman.

Secretary of Labor (Mitchell): former Assistant Secretary of the Army and labor-relations expert in several large organizations.

Secretary of Health, Education, and Welfare (Folsom): businessman and authority on social insurance and related fields.

Special Assistant on Disarmament (Stassen): former Governor and university president.

Ambassador to the United Nations (Lodge): former newspaperman and Senator.

Director of the Budget (Brundage): a public accountant.

Director of Office of Defense Mobilization (Flemming): university president.

Deputy Assistant to the President (Persons): Army, and school administrator.

Special Counsel to the President (Morgan): lawyer, former assistant legislative counsel to the House of Representatives.

Chairman of Civil Service Commission and President's Adviser on Personnel (Young): former dean of a graduate school.

Chairman of the Council of Economic Advisers (Burns): a university professor.

Assistant to the President on economic matters (Hauge): former economics professor and editorial writer for magazine.

It is hoped that this simple listing will help to restore a sense of proportion to those who are trying to sell the Amer-

ican public on an all-businessman tag for the Eisenhower
Administration.

Would most people believe you if you told them that the
incumbents of eight of the most important posts have been
in educational work? It is true: the President, the Special
Assistant on Disarmament, the Director of Defense Mobilization, the Secretary of Agriculture, the President's Adviser
on Personnel, the Deputy Assistant to the President, and the
President's two chief economic advisers. In addition, there
are two educators in Under Secretary positions: Labor, and
Health, Education, and Welfare, not to mention another college president, Kevin McCann, who is the President's assistant for preparation of speeches.

I suppose that no one could ever agree on the proper proportion of varying backgrounds for the top executive group,
and even if you could get agreement, you could not necessarily get the people to serve that you needed to round out
your pattern. The above analysis, however, should be sufficient to show that the make-up of the present Administration group is quite varied—certainly not so one-sided as to
give rise to a political issue—and that, for the most part,
where businessmen have been placed in key positions, they
are positions in which experience in business and finance is
directly relevant and valuable.

The Farming Business

When the farm problem is methodically discussed on the
merits, some people are inclined to give you a knowing wink
and say, "Sure, sure, but the real reason for all this special
attention to farmers is the number of Senators they elect,
isn't it?"

Let us start by dragging this matter of the relation of
special farm measures to politics right out in the bright white

light and taking a look at it. The entire debate in this area has often seemed to be carried on in an unreal atmosphere, because many people suspect that the reasons given for farm price supports are mere window dressing to cover up actions that have to be taken anyway for political reasons.

For example, one sometimes hears men in nonfarm businesses say, "Nobody supports my prices or guarantees me any income. Why should the farmer get guaranteed prices? It's all politics."

The question boils down to this: is there some feature of the farm business that so distinguishes it from other businesses that special governmental action on prices and markets for this one business may be justified on nonpolitical grounds?

(I feel rather strongly on this subject, as one who grew up in a farming community, worked for many years on farms, and at close range observed the farm problem unfold.)

True, the farm business is a business. The typical commercial farm involves a large investment, and has substantial current costs for materials, equipment and labor which are directly affected by what happens in nonfarm industry and commerce.

But in one important respect the farm business is unique.

It is the only business in which there are hundreds of thousands or millions of independent producers producing a product with a national (and even international) market and price.

There are other businesses that have a national market price, such as manufacturing and mining, but the number of producers is relatively small, and the size of at least some of the producers is apt to be very large.

And there are other business that have thousands of producers, such as residential construction or barbershops, but the market and the price are local.

But there are five million farmers, of whom at least two million are substantial commercial producers. And for the important commodities there is apt to be virtually one price.

This, in simplest terms, is why the farm business gets special attention.

If residential construction slumps in Seattle, or if the haircutting business languishes in Denver, some local builders and barbers are hurt, but it is not a national disaster.

But let the price of wheat drop in Chicago, and hundreds of thousands of farmers may face serious loss, even ruin.

And what does any one of those farmers have to say about what shall be the price of wheat in Chicago?

The individual farmer is at the mercy of a market price that is remote, complex and unpredictable.

Add to this the vagaries of the weather. A drought, an early freeze, or a spell of perfect weather can throw market calculations off either way. And that goes for weather not only in this country, but in other parts of the world.

Add to this the long lead time involved in many agricultural products. A manufacturer of pencils who sees a pencil surplus looming can cut down the rate of production of pencils. But when a farmer has seeded a hundred acres in corn and sees a surplus coming, he cannot pull out the seed and try something else. If he has sunk thousands of dollars into heifers, and sees a slump in beef prices coming, he cannot get his money back on the heifers. He is stuck with his commitment to the beef venture.

Add to this the remoteness of farmers from each other and their inherent disadvantage in trying to do anything in concert.

These uncertainties, and violent ups and downs, have always been a familiar feature of farming. But their impact on the modern farmer is somewhat different from their impact on his grandfather. Grandfather managed to sweat it out sometimes for several years with no profits, because he had no high sustained cash costs to keep up with. Grandson is loaded down with installment payments on the cornpicker, the combine and the last quarter section he bought so that he could have a big enough operation to support the cornpicker and the combine.

In short, he has the sustained costs of a regular business, but the market and his relation to it are quite different from those of other businesses.

It is at the points where the farmer is under his unique disadvantage that the government acts.

In the adjusting of production to the market, the farmer is under a unique disadvantage because there are five million of him trying to outguess a market which, even if it could be outguessed, might turn upside down at the last minute because of weather; therefore the government gets into the planning of volume of production.

In the helplessness of the individual producer in relation to the market, the farmer is also under a unique disadvantage; therefore the government intervenes with price supports.

In the inability of a single farmer to carry on research, the farmer is under a unique disadvantage; therefore the government carries on large-scale research, because the progress of this gigantic national industry is vital to everyone's welfare.

The modern history of agriculture, from the twenties on, demonstrates that the fortunes of farmers do not follow the same pattern as those of the economy generally. Agriculture follows its own pattern, and has its own problems.

It is not politics, then, but a conscientious attempt to apply distinctive measures to a distinctive business, that motivates and justifies the kind of special attention that agriculture has been accorded in the New Republican farm program.

President Eisenhower's Agriculture Message of 1956 has supplied a clear set of objectives for farm policy.

The weakness of farm policy in earlier years can be directly attributed to the absence of understood and consistent objectives—in other words, the failure to ask these questions, "Where are we ultimately heading? If governmental programs all work out exactly according to plan, what will be the final result? What do we *want* the final result to be?"

Is the objective:

a. to get as great production of farm products as possible, or
b. to make sure that farm income is at all costs kept at a high level in any given year, or
c. to restore a "sound" agriculture?

In the past, some policies seemed to be aimed at one objective, some at others, with the result that they sometimes canceled each other out and achieved no objectives at all.

a. High production at all costs, and hang everything else —this is the policy of war emergency.
b. High farm income at all costs, and hang what happens to sound agriculture in the meantime—this is the policy of shortsighted politics.
c. Sound agriculture at all costs, and hang what happens to farm income in the meantime—this is the policy of the pure theorist in agricultural economics.

The New Republican farm program has now charted a course toward plainly stated goals, all of which are consistent with each other. The most important of these objectives are the following:

1. Restore an undistorted market, by getting rid of surpluses.
2. Achieve a balanced rate of production, thus avoiding creating new surpluses, by adjusting price supports to the market.
3. Maintain farm income in the meantime under a system which will neither interfere with disposal of surplus nor distort production and produce more surplus.
4. Encourage the best possible land use and conservation practices.
5. Encourage the commercial family farm as the basic unit of our agriculture, by building up low-income farms toward this level, and by reducing financial aid to large industrial-type farm operations.

The difference between this program and the program in force during the Truman Administration centered around rigid 90-per-cent-of-parity price supports, may be summarized by resort once more to the three broad objectives set out at the start of this section:

The Truman Administration program aimed at (a) high production and (b) income support, at the expense of (c) sound agriculture.

The Eisenhower Administration program aims at (b) income support and (c) sound agriculture. High production, under present conditions, needs no encouragement; in fact, quite the opposite.

Before examining the affirmative New Republican farm principles, it is necessary to begin by asking what has been wrong in the Opposition's agricultural program. This requires us to review the story of the rigid 90-per-cent-of-parity plan.

Lest there be any misunderstanding on this score, let it be

said at once that there is nothing wrong with the concept of "parity" as such. The essential idea of parity is that of having a convenient index with which to relate farm prices and farm prosperity to general industrial prices and prosperity. Its practical purpose is to supply a guide and a tool to help ensure that the farmer does not get left behind in the procession of our economy. The point here is that the concept of parity can be applied in many ways other than the 90-per-cent-of-parity system.

The mechanism of the parity price support program begins with setting a parity figure, which is roughly a price for a commodity drawn from two past periods when farm prices were relatively favorable. Under a device known as the "non-recourse loan," the government "lends" the farmer an amount equal to a certain percentage, such as 90 per cent, of the parity price on his crop. For example, if the parity figure for wheat were $2.38 a bushel, the loan at 90 per cent of parity would be at the rate of $2.14 per bushel. If a farmer's crop were 10,000 bushels, his loan would therefore be about $21,400. If the actual market price proved to be less than $2.14 a bushel, the farmer would have the right to turn over his wheat to the government instead of repaying the loan. Therefore, if the actual market price were $2.00 a bushel, the farmer would receive at the hands of the government $1,400 above what he would have got on the open market.

This system had a small beginning during the depression when, in 1938, it was applied to several basic crops at a parity ratio between 52 and 75 per cent.

But the system in its full-blown form was essentially a war measure. During World War II the parity ratio was raised to 90 per cent, and applied to six basic commodities: cotton, wheat, corn, rice, tobacco and peanuts. Later the list was expanded, and at one time included as many as twenty commodities. At that time, it was provided that the system should extend only as far as two years beyond the close of hostilities.

It can readily be seen that this system was designed to do *two* things: support farm income *and* stimulate increased production. The heart of the postwar problem was that, of these two objectives, only one remained, which was that of maintaining farm income. As to the second objective, that of increased production, the situation was exactly reversed. We developed serious surpluses, but the nonrecourse loan system continued to apply stimulation of increased production just as if our problem were one of shortages.

When the Second World War ended, many other wartime devices acting directly upon prices and production were dismantled, but at this crucial point, when the process of adjustment back to natural market and price relationships should have been started, the fatal mistake was made of perpetuating into a time of peace and surplus a system designed to force added production in a time of war and shortage.

Right after the war, the Republican 80th Congress tried to make a start toward undoing this mistake and toward permitting adaptation of price supports to production needs, by installing a flexible plan calling for 60 to 90 per cent support of the basic commodities. But as soon as the Democrats were back in power, although the law on the books called for a flexible 75–90 per cent of parity, the parity figure was in fact frozen at 90 on the basics, with the nonbasics at similarly high figures.

The Truman Administration was temporarily saved from the consequences of having carried a wartime measure beyond the war period by the advent of another war, this time in Korea.

When in 1953 hostilities were ended in Korea, one of President Eisenhower's rewards was to be saddled with the accumulated weight of years of this erroneous farm policy.

The problem is low farm prices.

The reason for low farm prices is surpluses.

The reason for surpluses has been the incentive of high rigid price supports.

How then can the solution of a price problem caused by overproduction be a measure that was specifically designed to increase production?

Naturally, under such a fundamentally mixed-up approach, a lot of things went wrong. Attempts were made to hold down production by acreage controls. In many instances these attempts were thwarted. Sometimes the released acres were planted to other crops or used to raise livestock—thus merely shifting the overproduction problem to another commodity. Sometimes by concentrating on the most fertile acres and using fertilizers and improved techniques the farmers actually increased the volume of production although tilling fewer acres. For example, in 1955 the acreage allotments were supposed to reduce production to about ten million bales of cotton. Concentrated efforts by the farmers aided by good weather brought the final production to almost fifteen million. Meanwhile, the farmer's life was invaded by more and more annoying restrictions. And the public squirmed as it thought of seven billion dollars' worth of commodities resting and sometimes rotting in storage bins and the holds of old ships, running storage charges of a million dollars a day.

With all this effort, expense and trouble, the system did not even succeed in its objective of maintaining farm prices. The parity ratio dropped 19 percentage points from the

1951 peak to January, 1953. Per capita farm income dropped 7 per cent.

It is apparently one of the rules of the game of politics that the Administration in power gets blamed for everything that goes wrong during its tenure, no matter whose fault it is.

And so some people attacked the Eisenhower Administration for the operation of a farm program that it did not install and tried constantly to change. The unfairness of such an attack in 1953, based on prices that had been falling since 1951 under the inherited law, is quite obvious. Then an Administration bill permitting more flexible supports was passed in 1954. Although the new law was to take effect only as to the 1955 harvests, the 1954 price troubles (still flowing directly from the old law) were immediately blamed by some critics on the not-yet-operative change in policy. In fact, the real effect of the change can become apparent only over a period of years, particularly since, as President Eisenhower has said, "the new law is smothered under surpluses amassed by the old program."

Another interesting fact is that expenditures on stabilizing farm income have increased tremendously during the Eisenhower Administration. If the success of a farm program were in proportion to the generosity of government outlays on price supports, farm prosperity should have multiplied. The figures on cost of stabilizing farm prices and income are as follows:

1950:	$487 million	1953:	$330 million
1951:	$624 million	1954:	$963 million
1952:	$306 million	1955:	$1,300 million (est.)

Herculean efforts have been made to move the surpluses created by this program. The difficulties are severe. If you try to dispose of them within the country, the most elaborate precautions have to be taken to prevent any depressing of the domestic market—for otherwise, of course, the whole process would be self-defeating. If you try to dispose of them abroad by giving them to the hungry peoples of the world or by selling them at low prices, you run the risk of ruining the normal trade of friendly countries and turning them into enemies.

In spite of these limitations, farm surplus disposals have steadily increased, as follows:

1953:	$530 million
1954:	$1,424 million
1955:	$2,115 million

And yet, because of the rate of intake of new surpluses, the investment of the Commodity Credit Corporation in price-supported commodities increased by about a billion dollars during the year 1955.

This story of the failure of rigid price supports and the worsening problem of surpluses leads directly into the question: is there not some device, some combination, which will support farm income, and at the same time reduce surpluses and keep them reduced, so that eventually production, markets and prices will be able to achieve something approaching a balance?

There is such a device. It is a very ingenious device, and, used in conjunction with flexible supports, it promises to advance *all* of the Eisenhower Administration's farm objectives in the same operation.

This device is the Soil Bank.

It works this way. Suppose a farmer now has an acreage allotment of 160 acres of wheat. He will, without losing that full acreage allotment, be allowed to plant, say, 128 acres and put the other 32 into the "acreage reserve." This means that he agrees not to grow *any* crop or graze any stock on those 32 acres. In return, he is given a certificate whose value is equal to a percentage of the value of the crop he would normally have got from that 32 acres. The certificate is negotiable, and is redeemable in cash by the Commodity Credit Corporation, or in the particular crop from the government's stocks.

Thus, in the words of President Eisenhower, the plan "uses the surplus to reduce the surplus."

At the same time it maintains farm income. In fact, it adds even greater security in the form of a sort of insurance, since if there were a complete crop failure the farmer would have at least the income from his reserve acres.

This plan is suggested for wheat, cotton, corn and rice. Each of these has its special problems, and President Eisenhower's message contains a thorough list of special improvements in the program as to each, too detailed to go into here. As a result of these actions, it is expected that most crop carryovers should be down to normal levels in three or four years.

This part of the Soil Bank plan is called the "acreage-reserve program." There is a second part, called the "conservation reserve program." Under this plan, farmers are asked to contract voluntarily with the government to shift into forage, trees and water-storage cultivated lands most needing conservation measures. The government will pay a fair share of the costs of making this change of use, up to a specified maximum per acre. The farmer will agree to carry out sound soil and water conservation, and to withhold tillage or grazing for a specified period.

There is thus a sort of bonus in the Soil Bank plan, for, while dealing with the economic problem, it simultaneously helps substantially with a growing conservation problem resulting from the fact that many areas have been put into cultivation which good land use practices would require be kept in forage and trees. In the process, we protect and enrich our food-producing potential for whatever future demands may be put upon it. This same long-range objective is the subject of another complete program called the Great Plains Program, which is a many-sided attack on the special problems of land use created by the problems of wind and water erosion in the area between the prairies of the Central West and the Rocky Mountains.

The fifth objective of the New Republican farm program mentioned above is encouraging the commercial family farm unit as the basic unit of agriculture.

Under modern conditions, a farmer in order to have a standard of living comparable to that of his nonfarm counterpart needs a good-sized farm with a considerable capital investment in buildings and equipment. Rapid strides have been made in this direction. The size of farms has been increasing, and the increase in mechanization is almost unbelievable. The present capital value of the average farm is $27,000, and the average debt of farmers is only 11 per cent of their assets. Seventy-three per cent of farmers owned their own farms in 1950, as against 61 per cent in 1940 and 47 per cent in 1930. There are 4,300,000 tractors now as against 1,700,000 before Pearl Harbor. The number of grain combines has in the same period increased 318 per cent, the number of cornpickers 429 per cent, and the number of milking machines 233 per cent. This process has not stopped. Farm machinery purchases in 1955 were up 20 per cent compared with 1954.

The objective of encouraging the regular well-equipped good-sized family farm is approached from two sides. One is the program for low-income farm families known as the

Rural Development Program, started in 1955. This is a many-pronged attack on the causes of low income in certain rural areas, participated in by the Departments of Agriculture, Commerce, Health, Education, and Welfare, and Labor, as well as by state and local people and educational institutions. The other approach is the proposal to put a top dollar limit on the size of price support loans to any one individual or farming unit. The reason for this is that the real purpose of support legislation is to maintain income for farm families, not to write huge checks to large industrial-type enterprises which frequently compete with the very family farms whose prosperity is essential not only to our economic well-being but to the preservation of our traditional way of life.

There are many other features to the 1956 program, including abolition of the tax on gasoline used on farms, improved farm credit facilities, and a 25 per cent increase in research expenditures for such purposes as finding new uses for farm products, new markets and new distribution methods to cut down the growing margin between the retail price of food and the price the farmer gets.

One word of caution should be expressed: no farm program should be expected to eliminate farm price cycles. It may cushion them, put a brake on them, modify them or soften their effects. But market price is the built-in mechanism that regulates the volume of production of farm products and adjusts it to demand.

As every farmer knows who has been in the business for any length of time, the prices of farm products move in cycles in response to a demand-supply rhythm. In the case of hogs the cycle is about five years. In the case of chickens, it is about two. As for beef cattle, it is quite a bit longer.

The cycle works like this. At first, let us assume that hog prices are very high. What happens? A lot of people go into the hog business, and those already in the business increase their production to take advantage of the high prices. As a result, two things happen. An oversupply of hogs reaches the market at about the same time demand has been falling off because of the high price level. Housewives, seeing the high price of pork, get in the habit of buying beef or chicken. This coincidence of excessive supply and falling demand starts the cycle downward. Prices fall. Marginal producers get discouraged and get out of the hog business. Regular hog producers cut their production. The supply begins to decrease. Meanwhile, as a result of the low prices, the housewife once more begins to buy pork. Demand begins to firm up. The combination of increased demand and reduced supply starts the price movement upward again. Soon word gets around that raising hogs is a good bet once more. The marginal producers once more go in for hog raising. Hog producers increase their production, as they did in 1955—by 9 per cent. Prices hit a peak, as they did in 1954—at $25. Housewives again stop buying. The market is flooded with hogs, as it was in the fall of 1955. Prices drop to the low point of the cycle. And so it has been as long as anyone can remember.

The government can do a number of things about livestock prices, as it did in 1955 and 1956. It can go into the market and buy heavily, thus helping to firm up the price and start it back upward. It can provide inducements, as proposed under the Soil Bank plan, to reduce overproduction resulting from growing feed grains and grazing livestock on acres diverted from controlled crops. But, in farming as in any other business, it would be very harmful to regulate completely out of existence this kind of price cycle, even if you could, which you cannot.

Conclusion

To write about the relation of government to business prosperity is to run the risk of creating two misapprehensions, which must be emphatically negated here and now.

First, all this attention to expanded material well-being should not be taken to imply that economic satisfactions are the chief goal of either individual persons or the government. They are a means, not an end. The more successfully and efficiently we dispose of the problem of achieving food, clothing and shelter, the sooner and better we shall be able to live fully and richly the life of the spirit. So far as the government is concerned, in our tradition, it has never been given active responsibility for either the religious or the cultural life of our people.

But in the matter of employment, business cycles and general economic progress, the government has been given, both by such direct enactments as the Employment Act of 1946, and by the unmistakable expectations of today's voters, a clear assignment to watch over the scene and to act as necessary. We may as well face the obvious truth that, apart from international crises, the dominant topic of discussion in political campaigns is the state of business, in the broadest sense, including employment, the farm business, the cost of living and the prosperity of people.

In other chapters, such as those on labor and on the needs of people, we shall see that the segment of New Republican principle bearing on material prosperity will fall into its proper perspective among the other concerns and objectives of a well-rounded political philosophy.

The second caveat is this: the fact that this discussion happens to deal with the role of government in helping to achieve prosperity should not be taken to mean that the federal government, under this or any administration, in fact is *the cause of* prosperity.

The causes of our current good times are many. The basic cause is the fundamental rightness, for a vast, rich country like ours, of competitive private enterprise, with incentives for investment, effort and ingenuity. Then we must give much credit to the rapid growth in population, which continues to create consumer demands that provide a constantly increasing stimulus to new production. While the population has been growing, its composition also has been changing, notably in the increase in the ranks of the middle-income group. Consumer spending has come to dominate our economy, and this in turn flourishes because of good wages resulting in considerable measure from the efforts of the trade union movement, a going income-insurance system sustaining some purchasing power during unemployment, old age, widowhood or disability, up-to-date minimum wage and labor standards laws, and a sense of security for the future born of all these things. Skillful marketing and management play a big part, in such matters as control of inventory, systematic investment planning, and the development of mass markets to match mass production. Scientific and technological knowledge has surged ahead at an accelerating pace, supplying the indispensable technical means of carrying forward our industrial progress. The revolutionizing of the concept and sources of capital has been another liberating factor. The gradual and sometimes rapid rebuilding of the economies of friendly foreign countries has contributed no small part, for we have happily avoided the pitfall of supposing that an island of plenty can be maintained in the middle of a world of distress and depression.

All these forces, and many others, have been poured into one great stream to carry us to our present place.

But—and here is where government policy comes in—you have to have the right government attitudes, safeguards and auxiliary measures or all these things will not flourish. At practically every point in this list, there is something the government can do right, to bring out the best in that force, and something the government can do wrong, to deaden or distort that force. We have just seen what different government Administrations may do, wrong or right, about tax measures affecting investment, about credit control, about regulation of business, about fiscal management and so on. At other points we shall see how the right or wrong approach to such things as social insurance can have an important effect on the outcome. Government policy has to be right on labor relations, on scientific research and education, on foreign trade and aid, and all the rest.

When the government is right on these things, the country can prosper. When it is wrong, the country cannot prosper. In this sense, and in this sense only, there is a causal relation between government policy and business vigor, and in this sense it is proper for an Administration to take credit for prosperity.

4

The Labor Philosophy of
the New Republicanism

The labor philosophy of the New Republicanism is based upon the following principles:

1. Labor is practically everybody. Labor, in modern times, is not a downtrodden, miserable, unwashed mass of muscular malcontents who must be the special ward of a paternalistic government. Labor is all those who work for a living.

2. The aspirations of American working men and women are: to give, through their work, the highest and finest expression to their God-given abilities and talents; to maintain the dignity, the pride and the freedom that rightly belong to all free men; and to achieve a material standard of living within which these ideals of a good and useful life can, in ever-increasing measure, be realized for the worker and his family.

3. The free trade union movement should be encouraged, because it has been instrumental in raising both the dignity and the economic status of labor to their present levels, and since there is much more to be done in extending these benefits to others.

4. The most effective mechanism for achieving a proper

distribution of the fruits of production with a minimum of industrial strife is free collective bargaining, within a set of rules ensuring fairness to employers, to unions and to the individual persons represented. The role of the government is to ensure this fairness, to settle disputes about the rules governing the fair-bargaining process, to tender its good offices in the form of mediation and conciliation services to aid in arriving at agreement on the substance of a dispute, and only in rare cases of genuine national emergency to intervene more directly in a labor dispute.

5. The federal government does not and should not state a policy on what it thinks is labor's correct share in the benefits of our productivity. The maturity, experience and foresight of both management and labor representatives is such that the sharing worked out in their free bargaining will normally not damage the interest of the workers, the owners of the business or the public.

6. The ultimate object of concern of the New Republican philosophy of labor is the individual person. It is not the average welfare of men in the mass.

7. A complete system of income insurance, providing a portion of lost earnings to the worker or his family when wages are interrupted or stopped by involuntary unemployment, disability, old age or death, is not only valuable but indispensable in a modern mass-production cash-wage economy.

8. Although the government should avoid usurping the decisions and functions that are the proper sphere of collective bargaining, its role is not a negative one; it can and should discharge in modern times a wide range of positive functions serving to improve the well-being of workers— functions that by its nature the central government is in the best position to handle.

9. One of the most effective and convincing ways for an Administration to promote better labor standards is to be a good employer itself, and to set a good example in the areas where it has direct responsibility, such as in federal employment and in the District of Columbia.

10. Finally, New Republicanism declares that the Class Struggle is a lie. There is a surface contest—there always has been, always will be and always should be—between proprietors and workers over the price of the workers' services; but their ultimate interest is a mutual one: greater prosperity for all to share.

Who Is Labor?

The civilian "labor force" in December, 1955, numbered 66.6 million persons.

About 50 million of these were in nonagricultural employment. About 17 million of the 50 million were in manufacturing.

The unemployed in December numbered 2.4 million.

Women make up about a third of the work force.

About a fourth of the work force is organized. Three-fourths of the country's workers do not belong to unions.

The total figure for the labor force embraces all working people, including professional persons, farmers, executives, white-collar workers, self-employed persons, teachers, preachers, television actors, artists and unpaid family workers.

If you accept this "labor force" as being the same as "labor," you will find amply justified the opening assertion of this chapter: Labor is practically everybody.

There may have been, in the past, some inclination to create a stereotype which still flashes into the mind when one hears the word "labor." Perhaps it is only the result of hundreds of cartoons and murals, in which labor usually is depicted as a clean-cut young man in denim overalls and heavy work shoes; his neatly rolled-up sleeves reveal bronzed muscular forearms, slightly tensed as he grasps his trowel or hammer; his jaw is square, his gaze is clear, he never smokes, he is never bald, he never has a mustache, and he never ever wears glasses.

Perhaps this is all a legitimate piece of shorthand personification, just as Senators still wear string ties and wide-brimmed black hats in cartoons, even though the last two prototypes, Senators Connally and Hoey, are gone from the Senate.

Still, there is something important at stake here. Most people probably have their own trimmed-down mental picture of the range of the term "labor," and this may color an entire attitude on "the labor question."

When spokemen for labor are heard, they are quite understandably representatives of organized labor. Yet they would be the first to agree that "labor" is not limited to organized labor, which numerically still represents a minority of working people.

Should we rule out professional people? assistant editors? the personnel manager at the plant? the frail little man with thick glasses who tunes the piano? the girl on television who lisps out the praises of a cream shampoo?

But, in their way, they all work. And they work for wages or salaries or some kind of compensation which they use to buy food and clothing and shelter.

A little reflection will show that one cannot fairly expel from this category all but manual workers, since there are large and flourishing unions of clerks and television artists and teachers. Nor can you very well cut out supervisors, because, although at any given level the supervisor may look like the boss to those under him, there is usually another boss bossing him, and another boss bossing his boss. Eventually you may reach the point where the identity between boss and employer becomes so close that it no longer makes sense to speak of the man as "labor." But in any given case it may depend on the purpose involved. For example, top corporate executives are treated as employees under old-age and survivors insurance and in some workmen's compensation acts. At that point, the corporation president and the furnace man stand side by side in interest, so far as their personal rights under the act are concerned. Even the self-employed now have a stake in the social security system. The personnel manager may lose his job and need unemployment insurance as badly as the next man. Bad safety practices that get the plant blown up will blow up the third vice president along with the rest of the help. And, although many of these members of the labor force will never fit into the labor side of a collective bargaining scene, still they all have in common that universal interest: getting a raise.

It is interesting to recall that, in the history of the trade union movement, there was a time when the positions were somewhat reversed. The craft unions, tracing their lineage to the guilds of the Middle Ages, which were exclusive brotherhoods carrying considerable prestige and power, resisted for many years any attempt to bring unskilled labor within the orbit of the trade union movement. It was the monumental achievement of John L. Lewis in one lifetime to establish firmly the unionization of unskilled workers. But it was not until 1955, with the final AFL-CIO merger, that the process of bringing unskilled workers into a permanent association with the craft unions was completed.

The point of all this is merely to jog us all loose from old mental habits when the subject of "labor" is mentioned. A surprising number of people, without thinking much about it, are apt to feel that labor is something you are either for or against. At the extreme, one sometimes encounters the kind of person who, in a political discussion, will unconsciously seem to classify "labor" as just one more minority, with a certain vote, somewhat like the displaced Poles or the tung-nut growers.

The only cure for this is to keep reminding ourselves that labor is practically everybody, and that it makes little sense to say that "labor thinks this" or "the labor vote will go such-and-such a way."

The people composing this labor force will group and regroup in various patterns of mutual interest, depending on the issue at stake. I have heard an injured corporation president cry out bitterly against the inadequacy of workmen's compensation; I have had letters from proprietors of small independent service establishments demanding to know why a proprietor cannot be brought under unemployment compensation; I have seen a highly paid consulting professional architect killed on a project because of a bad safety violation. At such times, and for such purposes, the corporation executive, the self-employer and the professional man were as much identified in interest with labor as any member of the labor force could be. The same is much more true of groups like teachers, stenographers, nurses, salaried lawyers and federal bureaucrats, who are a long way from the stereotype of "labor," but who usually have as much right and need to be in that category as anyone.

In short, *labor is not a class.*

The second important fact about labor is that it has changed markedly in recent times and is still changing. This is one more example of the theme stated at the outset: that most of the key facts have changed since the conventional opposition ideologies became fixed.

The most important change is the result of technological advances in industry, including what is now popularly referred to as automation. The effect has been that unskilled labor is giving way to semiskilled, and semiskilled to skilled, while skilled workers are moving into the range of technicians and engineers.

The number of unskilled workers in 1910 accounted for 36 per cent of the work force.

In 1950 this percentage had dropped to 20.

In 1910 semiskilled workers represented 15 per cent of the labor force.

In 1950 the percentage of semiskilled was 22½.

Thus, the relative number of unskilled workers has been practically cut in half, while the relative number of semiskilled has grown by half.

There has been much talk and controversy about the effects of automation; but one thing seems quite clear: it will accelerate this process of raising the skill level of the work force.

Just as steam power and the industrial revolution freed us from dependence on human muscle power and arduous physical strain, so automation will begin to displace many kinds of semiskilled labor and substitute a requirement for skilled technicians.

As this process continues and accelerates, the stereotype of labor as a sweating straining mass of humanity becomes more and more unrealistic, and the political theories that are in any degree consciously or unconsciously constructed around this stereotype become progressively more obsolete and dangerous.

This same process of technological change, in the form of agricultural mechanization, has produced another revolutionary shift—that in the relative size of the agricultural and nonagricultural work force. From 1932 to 1953 the number of persons employed in manufacturing increased from 6.7 million to 17.2 million—almost trebled. In the same span of years, the number of people in the farm labor force dropped from about 10.2 million to 6.6 million. Employment in service industries doubled, rising from about 2.7 million to 5.5 million. The total number of people employed in all work, agricultural or nonagricultural, rose from 39 million to 62 million, and by the second half of 1955 was approximating a rate of 65 million—about ten times the farm work force.

This shift has many meaningful implications, not the least of which is its political significance. There are many sections of the country which have thought of themselves as being overwhelmingly agricultural in character, so much so that their representatives have sometimes thought that typical "labor problems" are no concern of theirs. However, even if you take as an example a state like South Dakota, which most people would think of as almost exclusively an agricultural state, you will find that there are now more people in the nonagricultural work force than there are in farm employment and farm self-employment combined.

With the onrush of mechanization, farm labor itself has greatly changed, and has required an increasing ability to handle more and more elaborate and expensive machinery.

Once it is fully realized that labor is not a class, it will also be clear that "labor's" greatest gains will come, not by a partisan fight to get something at the expense of some other group, but by the increased well-being of the people as a whole, since "labor" is so nearly identical with the people as a whole.

What Does Labor Want?

Some time ago a poll was taken among retail store employees asking each one what he considered most important of all in his relation to his work and his employer. The results were published in the April, 1939, *Personnel Journal.*

First of all, the worker wanted recognition as a human being and an individual. Second, he wanted the satisfaction of doing good work that he understood and that gave him some degree of self-expression. He wanted, in other words, things that were personal and spiritual more than things that were exclusively material. Wages were rated third.

Of course, this assumes that a man has a good steady job. It is not much use talking about self-expression and spiritual satisfaction to a man who is out of work.

But the far-reaching importance of this attitude lies in the way it once more gives the lie to the assumptions of some old-fashioned reformers and revolutionaries. Karl Marx laid down, as one of the foundation stones of his doctrine, the principle of economic determinism. This assumption that human motivations are ultimately material has in some degree filtered into the ideas of many people who have no truck with Marx or Communism as such. On the employee side, it is apt to lead to the assumption that the success of labor's efforts is to be measured mechanically and quantitatively in the rate by which the cents-per-hour figure goes up. From the employer's side, it may mean that the employer believes he has discharged all his obligations to his employees when he has paid them the requisite cash wage. And from the side of public servants, reformers, social workers and theorists, it may lead to the danger of placing too much emphasis on average quantitative physical welfare.

Of course, it would be fatuous to pretend to be so high-minded as to treat wages as a sordid detail. That is not the idea. Good wages, respectable working conditions, reasonable hours, protection of status, seniority and security—all these are what you build upon in order to reach the higher nonmaterial aims. Here and there a great artist may be the by-product of starvation in a garret, and a great philosopher may live in a cave and eat berries; but, taking it all in all, you will usually find that a generally high level of culture and civilization is made possible by a firm economic underpinning.

There is widespread evidence on all sides that this supramaterial view of labor's aims and management's responsibilities is becoming established in this country. The great labor federations are devoting much time and money to civic improvements, education, medical and psychiatric care and research, and other public-service enterprises. The employers are constantly engaged in self-examination in such matters as job satisfaction and personal relations within the plant. Just as "automation" dominates technical conferences nowadays, so "human relations" dominates the personnel conferences.

But what effect does this view of the importance of status and self-expression have on government and political theory?

It rules out the "mass" concept of people. This has a practical effect on exactly how you construct such things as social security laws and income tax statutes.

It similarly renders presumptuous any assumption that labor is a tractable herd that can be led around by the nose with promises of special material concessions. This assumption is the greatest affront imaginable to people who are striving to assert their own personalities and their own destinies.

It means that there must be much more emphasis by government and everyone else on affording training, apprentice-ship and educational opportunities that will enable every person to realize the best that is in himself.

It raises to a high level of priority all those projects that are aimed at removing prejudices and discrimination which insult the self-respect of competent workers. Discrimination against mature workers is not only an economic hardship to them; it is apt to be a crushing blow to their pride and per-sonality. It hardly needs to be said that the same is true of racial discrimination in employment. Refusal to hire women in suitable occupations, or to provide equal pay for equal work, carries with it the same combination of material dis-crimination and humiliation.

One can judge, then, where an Administration or political movement stands on this matter by how actively it lives up to these principles.

As to its over-all concept of labor, the New Republicanism has repeatedly made it clear that it does not isolate labor as a class. Politically, it has expressed its confidence that all working people will individually consult their own con-sciences and express their sovereignty as citizens.

As to some of the specific activities mentioned: the first thoroughgoing effort in history is under way in the U. S. De-partment of Labor to analyze the skills of the nation's work force and the way the skill potentialities of more workers can be brought out through a greatly accelerated nation-wide training drive; the government's biggest attack on the problem of unjustified road blocks to employment of mature workers has been launched; President Eisenhower's Com-mittee on Government Contracts has quietly made more progress in eliminating racial discrimination in employment than has been made for many years past; legislation calling for equal pay for women is part of the Administration program; a Cabinet committee on migratory farm workers is making real progress in improving the dignity and community acceptance, along with the physical welfare, of this long-neglected group; a lively and effective program to restore self-respect along with employment to the physically handicapped is being constantly expanded, with the aid of such direct measures as the Vocational Rehabilitation Act of 1954, which permitted the amount of rehabilitation to be multiplied.

There is a thread that runs through all this. It is a profound concern for the legitimate aspirations of individual people to earn and hold their rightful place in society and in the esteem of their fellows, and to achieve the happiness that goes with leading a useful and creative life.

Trade Unionism

The New Republicanism is in favor of trade unionism.

In his telegram on the occasion of the opening of the Teamsters' Building in Washington, President Eisenhower said:

Strong, dedicated, democratic trade unionism is one of the bulwarks of our American way of life. Our democracy and our economy both make possible and draw strength from free trade unions.

This quotation is adduced here because we are dealing with an area in which assertions have to be displaced by evidence. There have been occasional reckless statements, made for some immediate political purpose, that the Eisenhower Administration is somehow unfriendly to unions. This is untrue.

The truth lies both in the words just quoted, and in the deeds that are recounted throughout this chapter.

As to results: it has been during the New Republican

regime that organized labor has reached its most satisfactory position in history. (Financially, the unions have made remarkable strides, because of pension funds, higher wages and smaller drains on the treasury for strike benefits. Membership is the highest it has ever been. Success in collective bargaining has been conspicuous, in that wage gains substantially beyond the increase in cost of living have been achieved for the first time in years, and other benefits such as supplementary unemployment insurance and pensions have made great advances. To top it all off, the merger of the AFL-CIO has taken place.

Of course, it will be said that the Administration can hardly take credit for all this—especially the merger. That is not really the point. The point is that when an Administration has stated its support of trade unionism, backed it up with an array of legislation and administrative action favorable to labor beyond anything seen in fifteen years, and presided over a period which produced the highest wages, highest take-home pay, highest real income, highest union treasuries, highest union memberships, lowest industrial accidents, highest consumer spending and highest gains in fringe benefits in history—the working man might well say, "If this is not prolabor, what is?"

Labor unions are valuable for many reasons. Most important is their function of uniting the strength of employees for bargaining purposes. This brings about not only a higher level of wages than the individual worker could ordinarily negotiate for himself but a more uniform level, and a structure that is balanced between cash wages and various other benefits such as vacations, medical benefits and the like. Unions also provide a mechanism through which everyday grievances can be presented to the employer and settled.

In addition, unions provide labor market information for their individual members. In some occupations, the union actually does most of the work of finding and providing jobs, as in the case of some building trades and the maritime unions' hiring halls. Moreover, unions keep their members constantly informed of their legal rights under various labor and social insurance statutes.

Not least of the union's values is its effect of giving the worker a sense of belonging and of the confidence and status that goes with association. In a large industrial establishment, it is no longer possible for a single worker to have much contact with his employer, or much feeling of having any chance to get acquainted with him or talk things over with him. This lack has to some extent been filled by the union, which gives the worker some sense of effectively communicating with his employer and having something to say about his own fortunes.

These are some of the benefits of unionism from the members' point of view. Unions make many other contributions as well, in promoting legislation, in combating Communism at home and overseas, in philanthropic, civic and educational activities, and in long-range economic research.

It is worth while to rehearse these simple facts about unions, because there are many people in this country whose mental association with the word "union" is almost invariably "strike." At some time a strike has affected the particular person unpleasantly by making him walk upstairs when the elevators were not running, or by complicating his transportation when the streetcars stood idle, or by depriving him of his favorite paper for a time. Or he may have a vivid mental picture of one of those rare labor disputes in which cars get turned over and firearms get discharged, forgetting that this sort of thing has happened only a few times out of hundreds of major strikes in recent years.

Those who work with these matters every day realize that labor unions are a stabilizing influence in labor relations, and under the kind of mature leadership now becoming prevalent can be good for employer and employee alike.

There is an important correlation between this New Republican view on unions and the policy of governmental withdrawal from interference in private affairs.

Note that it is where labor is unorganized that the government must step in with minimum wage laws and other labor standards legislation. To the extent that unions take over the job of raising these wage standards, the government can withdraw from the field. There is thus a clear internal consistency within the principles of New Republicanism on this point.

Putting the "Free" in "Free Collective Bargaining"

The central idea of unionism was and is to substitute collective for individual strength in bargaining on wages and conditions of employment. It is too obvious for argument that a single employee bargaining with a great corporation, or even with a moderately small employer, is under a disadvantage, except perhaps in time of serious labor shortage. Some employers might contend that there is no need for bargaining at all, since they will voluntarily pay good wages and provide good working conditions. But, whatever might be said of a particular employer here or there, the history of labor shows that generally improvements in the status of labor have had to be won by bargaining. Once you concede that bargaining is necessary, and that individual bargaining is inadequate, and that collective bargaining is therefore necessary, you come inescapably to the conclusion that the key to the whole matter is to ensure that collective bargaining is conducted under the fairest possible circumstances.

The role of the federal government in this development has varied. In the earliest stages, the government was sometimes found on the side of the employer, suppressing what we would now readily accept as legitimate collective action. Sometimes the law of conspiracy was pressed into service, or restraint of trade was alleged; even the concept of riot was sometimes resorted to. It was many years before the Clayton and Norris-LaGuardia Acts clearly laid down the rule that the labor of human beings was not an article of commerce and that combinations in respect to it were not within the Anti-Trust Laws.

During the thirties, the pendulum swung to the other side, and the government for a number of years threw its weight on the side of the growing union movement. It was generally accepted that the original Wagner Act was weighted in favor of the unions, on the theory that, in the stage of unionization so far attained, the balance of economic power was on the employer's side, especially in view of the very high rate of unemployment. For example, the act forbade a number of unfair labor practices by employers, with no corresponding prohibition of unfair labor practices by unions. A period of lively union growth ensued, at the rate of about a million members a year until 1939. The act was in part responsible; the formation of the CIO was another important cause. Another period of marked growth was during World War II, due largely to the marked increase in employment. About six million more members were added during the war.

By 1947, it was thought by some that the strength of unions, demonstrated both in membership growth and in a series of dramatic and prolonged strikes, had reached the point where the weighting of the act in favor of unions was no longer necessary. The Labor-Management Relations Act was rewritten with the announced intention of bringing it as much as possible into balance, without giving a statutory advantage to either party. Thus, to offset the employer's unfair labor practice provisions, there were inserted unfair labor practice provisions applicable to unions. But, when one sets out to swing a pendulum back, he seldom succeeds in making it stop right in the middle. Some think the act is still weighted in favor of employees; some think it is now too much proemployer. An anti-Communist oath was exacted of union leaders, but not of employers. In the controversial section 14(b), while the union shop was recognized, states were given the right to pass laws on union security that were more unfavorable to labor, without a similar option to pass laws that were more favorable.

The Labor-Management Relations Act is undoubtedly not the perfectly balanced instrument it should be, nor is it likely ever to become so. Attempts to modify it have invariably run into an impossible tangle. On the one hand, a whole slate of proposals is lined upon the labor side, ranging from repeal of the Taft-Hartley changes through a long list of amendments favorable to organized labor. From the other side comes a barrage of amendments which would ban the union shop, and turn all labor relations over to the states with full authority to ban strikes and picketing if they wished. Moderate, selective, carefully prepared corrections in the worst features of the act, such as the set of amendments proposed by the Eisenhower Administration regularly every year since 1954, get lost in the cross fire.

The practical question therefore becomes: assuming matters continue to stand approximately as they are, have we got a reasonably workable framework within which to carry on free collective bargaining? The best answer seems to be, once more, results. Negotiations of unprecedented complexity, involving such far-reaching developments as supplementary unemployment benefits, have been carried through with a minimum of strife. Some "right-to-work" laws, narrowing the union security standards of the federal act, have been passed, chiefly in the less industrial states, but the spread of these acts appears to have stopped.

Whatever the potential dangers of the Taft-Hartley Act from labor's point of view might be on paper, they do not seem to have materialized in such a way as to damage or hold back the labor movement in any serious degree in almost ten years of experience.

This being so, the New Republican position became this: that the bargaining setting and the bargaining position of the parties was sufficiently fair and balanced to make it both unnecessary and indeed harmful for the federal government to interfere in a labor negotiation or dispute, except in clear national emergencies such as the strike at the Oak Ridge atomic plant. It should be clearly understood that this was neither an obvious nor an easy line to take up and maintain. For many years, under Presidents Roosevelt and Truman, the ultimate resort in labor matters had been to the White House, and labor negotiations had been conducted often under the shadow of possible White House intervention. The climax came with President Truman's illegal seizure of the steel industry in 1952. There was thus a pattern to be broken, and a new conviction to be instilled in both employers and unions that resort to the federal government could not be substituted for good-faith bargaining.

In the stress of strikes like that on the Louisville and Nashville Railway and in the Southern Bell System in 1954, with loss and inconvenience to individuals, businesses, employers and employees in the area, it is perhaps understandable that ultimately not only unions but employers and Governors were demanding that the President of the United States step into the dispute. President Eisenhower put the negotiators on their own resources, with the aid of the regularly established federal mediation services, and the disputes were settled.

Let us suppose, for a moment, that the Secretary of Labor and the President had officially thrown their weight into the balance. What would have happened some months later, when one of the most difficult negotiations in the history of collective bargaining—that on the demand for a guaranteed annual wage—took place between the automobile manufacturers and the United Automobile Workers? Hard on the heels of this contract came the big steel negotiations, followed by many other industries any one of which, if shut down for long, would really have left a critical situation. If a pattern of government intervention had been set, can anyone doubt that it would have been much harder to bring off these delicately balanced negotiations as successfully, promptly and peacefully as was done?

Here again, the test of the rightness of a policy is results. The year 1954, in which the full implications of this policy had had time to take effect, saw less man-hours lost by strikes than any year since World War II. In some ways 1955 was even more remarkable, since time loss due to strikes ran at a rate lower than any postwar year except 1954 and 1951, in spite of the fact that there was a succession of contract renewals in the largest industries, such as automobiles, steel, copper, glass, electrical equipment and many others, and in spite of the fact that the guaranteed annual wage was up for negotiation in many of them. Adding to the significance of this record is the high level of production, wages and profits, which sometimes provides a setting for protracted labor disputes, because the union treasuries can afford a strike and workers are not so much worried about their jobs as in shakier times. The fact that 1955 passed, then, as a year of relative labor peace is evidence of the wisdom of the Eisenhower Administration's labor dispute policy.

Of course it would be improper for the Administration to take a major share of credit for this state of affairs; the major credit belongs to the unions and employers who amicably worked out their own differences. But here, as elsewhere, although the Administration may perhaps not actively cause the satisfactory result, it does deserve credit in the sense that if it had not courageously pursued its avowed new line of policy, the private efforts would undoubtedly have been much less successful.

What Is Labor's "Fair Share"?

Should it be an objective of government to define the fair share of labor in the product of our economy and, if necessary, to see that labor gets that fair share?

There are those who think so, and who would say that any Administration which fails to undertake this assignment has no real labor policy at all.

This technique of talking about the "fair share" of this or that segment of our society is by no means confined to labor. It is even more familiar in discussion of farm income.

And domestic industries do not want to destroy imports; they just want their "fair share" of the domestic market. Truckers do not mean to put railroads out of business, nor railroads put truckers out of business; each asks no more than his "fair share" of the transportation traffic.

We will all agree. Everyone should have his fair share. The

next question is: who decides what is the fair share of each competing interest?

It cannot very well be the interested party whose share is at stake.

Who then? There are not many impartial judges to choose from. It could hardly be the clergy; perhaps a panel of university economics professors, but it may be doubted whether they could enforce their verdict, even if they could agree on one, which is unthinkable.

And so, as often happens, we come back to the federal government, which has presumed impartiality, presumed wisdom and actual power.

The end of this road, then, is that the government decides what shall be the rewards and enjoyments of those within its jurisdiction.

Assume the government is to make this decision; how does it figure the fair share?

The use of a past period, as in farm parity, would undoubtedly be rejected by labor, on the ground that labor has never yet reached its proper relative share in any past period.

Deprived of a past bench-mark to base a parity formula on, one is thus left with the necessity of calculating, in the abstract, how much of the goods the economy produces should go to reward labor, how much to reward investors, how much to reward inventors and promoters, and how much to be plowed back into plant and expansion.

Perhaps such a calculation is possible on some over-all basis, although again one could hardly expect much agreement on it. But what is utterly beyond anyone's calculation is what those ratios should be for a given industry, or given state of the business cycle, or a given area of the country, or certainly for a particular plant. Even a slight approach to this sort of activity would soon substitute government for private decisions at every crucial point in our economic life.

The New Republican view on this is that when you have good business and union leadership imbued with a conviction that their ultimate interest is a mutual one—a prosperous country with more for all to share—and when you have a working system of free collective bargaining with no chance for overreaching by either side, you will produce the most satisfactory distribution of the nation's goods that can be achieved, while at the same time constantly increasing everyone's share.

This last factor is most important, because it distinguishes our philosophy from that of some of the more extreme left-wing reformers. Keynes once pointed out in a letter to Shaw that what the Marxians were aiming at was not really to pull everyone up to the level of the most prosperous, but to drag everyone down to the dead level of the most miserable. The difference was well expressed by Abraham Lincoln, who was not unaware of the beginnings of Marxian thought in his time, in his famous saying: "Let not him who is houseless pull down the house of another, but let him work diligently and build one for himself."

In this homely example lies the answer to our question; translated into economic and political terms, it simply means that top priority should be given to increasing the total product and second priority to the question of sharing. If both men are houseless, relative sharing between them may be fairer than before, in that there are two miserable men rather than one. But if the new house is built, the ultimate result is also a fair share for each, *and* a house for each.

Again, results bear out the view that his process in practice is favorable to labor.

Taking "shares" in the literal sense of the portion of national income going to major segments in the economy, one finds that while total national income approximately trebled between 1929 and 1954, compensation of employees more than quadrupled. Over the same period, the aggregate income of business and professional entrepreneurs trebled. Rental income doubled, net interest income only increased 50 per cent, and corporate profits trebled.

In the last century, the *real* income of labor, in the sense of ability to buy goods and services, has multiplied four times over.

The conclusion is clear: it would have been most unfortunate for labor if any fair share had been fixed in the past—even one which might have seemed generous at the time; and it is better now to continue to stress free bargaining and to avoid abstract talk about ensuring fair sharing.

Objective: the Worker Himself

Labor matters of concern to the government can be divided under two great headings: collective and individual.

Individual labor problems are those having to do with the worker's safety, health, economic security, job placement, apprenticeship and training, income insurance, and individual wages, hours or working conditions, whether he belongs to a union or, as is true of three-fourths of the work force, does not belong to a union.

Collective labor problems are those associated with the collective bargaining process: the right to form unions and recruit members without molestation, the process of establishing the right of a union to represent a bargaining unit, the framework of fair collective bargaining in good faith, and the prevention of unfair labor practices.

But in both categories, the final objective is the same: the well-being of the worker. The rights of organization, representation and bargaining do not exist for the benefit of unions as such, any more than corporation statutes exist for the benefit of corporations as such. They all exist for the people that make them up.

Acceptance of this simple but often-forgotten truth can have some everyday consequences for governmental activity.

It helps to keep a proper scale of relative importance between various issues, for one thing. No one will deny that amendment of the Taft-Hartley Act is important, and would result in an improvement in the collective relations of labor and management. But, when time and resources have to be budgeted to produce the maximum good for the workers of the country, and when two million people are being injured at work annually, and thousands of older workers are suffering from discrimination, and income insurance laws throughout the country are below proper standards, and skills shortages are a block to present progress and a threat to the future, and pockets of stubborn unemployment are still persisting in some areas, and thousands more handicapped workers could be rehabilitated and placed, and wages and hours and conditions of labor for unorganized workers are still substandard in many places and industries, and much of the fate of the Free World hangs on the effectiveness of overseas activities in the field of labor—it may well be concluded that the entire legislative concern of the Department of Labor, and the bulk of the time of the Labor Committees in Congress, and the available space for labor news and discussions in the public media of information, should not be monopolized by the Taft-Hartley Act. A few years ago, there was danger of this happening. Anyone might be forgiven for getting the impression that the entire world of labor lay in that act, and that everything else could well stand aside until the wrongs in that act were put right. It took a couple of years to restore a proper sense of proportion, but this restoration has made it possible to develop and move forward a wide range of legislative enactments beneficial to working people which never could have had a hearing if the obsession with Taft-Hartley had continued.

Labor Policy Begins at Home

The federal government has direct responsibility for the labor standards applied to two major groups of workers: federal employees and people within the District of Columbia.

It is necessary to do no more than list the actions of the New Republican Administration during its short tenure to make the point that, if example speaks louder than exhortation, this is a prolabor record indeed.

1. Unemployment insurance was extended to federal workers for the first time, by the Republican Congress.
2. A "fringe benefit" bill was passed, bringing a number of fringe benefits to federal workers, which were becoming increasingly commonplace among private employers.
3. A large pay increase for federal workers was put through.
4. A group life insurance plan for federal workers was instituted.
5. A health and welfare plan was worked out and is pending.
6. Work injuries among federal workers were sharply reduced.
7. A bill to charge work-injury compensation costs directly to the employing agencies as a stimulus to safety activity was introduced.
8. A long-range reform of workmen's compensation pro-

cedures for federal workers was undertaken, to give them a hearing on their claims and judicial review.

9. Unemployment insurance benefits for the District of Columbia were raised 50 per cent, and a number of other improvements made.

10. A complete insurance system for nonoccupational disability in the District of Columbia was prepared and introduced for the first time, with the backing of President Eisenhower.

11. An increase in workmen's compensation benefits for residents of the District, and for longshoremen, from a maximum of thirty-five to fifty dollars a week, was proposed and introduced.

These actions speak for themselves. The federal government is becoming one of the best of the country's large employers, and the District of Columbia is on its way to becoming one of the best jurisdictions in respect to labor legislation.

The Class Struggle Lie

Karl Marx taught that there was, between workers and employers, a relentless class struggle which was practically one of the laws of nature.

In this doctrine, he was describing and distorting into a vicious formula the facts of life as they appeared to him more than a hundred years ago in a Europe that was passing through the stormiest, rawest, most painful period of the evolution of the factory system, the industrial revolution and the rise of modern capitalism. This new economic structure was being superimposed upon a social structure in which class and caste were taken for granted, in which the man who worked was thought of as a "villein" and definitely inferior, and in which the man who did no work was a "gentle-man."

The employer, according to the Class Struggle theory, was the natural enemy of the employee, and it followed that the mission of labor was to fight the employer in every possible way and, if possible, destroy him. Workers imbued with this idea might even, at the height of a bitter dispute, bomb the very plant or smash the very machinery whose operation was their livelihood.

From the employer's point of view, the effect of this theory was to view labor as a commodity like any other cost of doing business. The idea was to buy labor as cheaply as possible, get as much work out of employees as possible over as long a day and week as the human frame could conceivably bear, and when workers collapsed, or got sick or injured, or were too old to work, throw them on the scrap heap exactly as you would a broken or worn-out piece of machinery.

In the Marxian theory, it was easy to identify and segregate the two great warring forces: Capital and Labor.

Capital was the rich, idle individual who lived on the earnings of his great fortune, and who has been pictured for us in innumerable cartoons since that time sitting on large bags of gold, wearing a silk top hat and smoking an enormous cigar.

Labor was the poor man with nothing to sell but his labor, with no property and no stake in the economic system, and with nothing to lose but his chains.

Now, when you try to apply this dichotomy to the American scene in the mid-twentieth century, you run up against one awkward fact: we are almost all of us Labor, and we are almost all of us Capital. This makes it difficult to stage much of a Class Struggle.

In the first part of this chapter, we have examined the fact that most people in this country are labor in the sense that they work for a living. How many people of working age and in good health do you know, rich or poor, who do not work regularly?

A visitor from France as long ago as 1897 wrote:

> There must be either a vein of duplicity, or a streak of insanity (according to Americans) in a man of forty-five who is willing to live on his income. In England polite snobbery dictates the question: "How are you amusing yourself?" In America polite snobbery dictates the question: "What (work) are you doing?"

Just as most of us are Labor, so are we most of us Capital. Profound changes have taken place in the sources of Capital since the days of Marx, and, as is much less widely understood, even since the early thirties.

Of course, we all know that capital is not nowadays furnished by a few great individual fortunes. We usually assume that capital comes from public issues of stocks and bonds, which are traded on the stock exchanges. The fact is that, in recent years, public securities issues have fallen to third place among the sources of capital. The two larger sources are the reserves of the great insurance companies, trust funds, pension funds and the like, and withheld earnings of corporations.

The holdings of the insurance companies and trust funds represent, in effect, the equities of millions upon millions of ordinary people in life insurance, pension plans and other types of savings. The extent to which this "broadens the base" of our capital structure may be seen from the fact that the owners of life insurance alone total 104,340,000.

The wide dispersion of the stocks held directly by the public is a well-known story. In the case, for example, of the largest railroad, the largest utility and the largest industrials, the largest stockholder owns less than 1 per cent. A.T. & T. has over a half-million stockholders—more stockholders than employees, in fact. U.S. Steel has almost as many stockholders as employees—200,000.

Of course, there are still some great personal fortunes and accumulations of capital. But even they, to some extent, have become institutionalized in the great Foundations. And one can only speculate about what Marx would say if he could witness the spectacle of these last great repositories of family fortunes being investigated by a Congressional Committee on suspicion of left-wing tendencies.

There is a second profound change in capital which has had far too little emphasis. This has to do with the great new source of capital called "withheld earnings of corporation."

Many people, when they think of common stock dividends, have the idea that what happens is something like this: a corporation at the end of the year adds up its profits; it then pays the interest on its bonds and debentures, and the fixed dividends on its preferred. After that it takes what is left, divides it by the number of common stockholders, and sends out dividend checks accordingly.

Nowadays, what actually happens in the major companies seems to be quite different. The company figures out a rate of return on its common which is sufficient to keep the stockholders reasonably happy, maybe around 6 per cent, and declares regular dividends of this amount whether its actual profits are 10 per cent or 20 per cent. Stockholders sometimes suspect that the dividend checks saying "This represents your regular quarterly dividend of 30c per share, etc." are printed up in quantity years in advance, since they do not seem to depend much upon the current rise and fall of profits. What happens to the excess? It is plowed back into the company for expansion, modernization and development, and for some years these "withheld earnings" have actually outstripped new public securities as a source of capital. In the first three quarters of 1955, *half* of all corporate earnings were retained rather than distributed.

The significance of this development on labor relations is tremendous. It always used to be assumed that the contest over fair sharing of the fruits of the enterprise was a strictly two-way affair. Labor would look at the size of the profits and argue that the owners were getting more than their due share of the profits, and could afford to share more with the employees in the form of increased wages. In other words, there was an assumption that the pot was going to be split two ways—between wages on the one hand, and dividends on the other.

What really happens in many of the large corporations is that the pot is split three ways, with the dividend figure remaining relatively stable. The withheld earnings amount is the figure that will frequently expand or contract according to the ability of labor to obtain a larger share through larger wages.

What this means is that when a corporation does make large profits, the result is generally not that a number of capitalists get a lot of loose cash to spend in riotous living; rather, the effect will probably be that the company will have a useful source of capital for expansion and for strengthening its competitive position. This means more jobs, better and more productive machinery, *resulting in higher man-hour productivity and thus higher wages,* and greater job security within the plant because of its improved competitive status.

This is a far cry, then, from the Marxian picture of Mr. Moneybags sitting on his sacks of gold, while the workers try to extract as much of it as they can, figuring that every

dollar they get away from him is just one less dollar for him
to spend on luxurious idleness.

The mutuality of interest of management and labor which
is the cornerstone of New Republican labor philosophy is
thus not the result of some intellectual or ideological conviction; it is rather the natural outgrowth of the actual sharing
of capital and actual sharing of labor which characterizes
our economy. This in turn reflects our attitude of respect for
work, respect for the individual person, respect for property,
ease of mutual understanding and sense of common destiny.

This labor philosophy requires and produces a new kind of
labor leader and a new kind of employer. The modern labor
leader concerns himself with the problems of the employer,
such as costs, markets, competition and future prospects,
and when he comes to settle a dispute, the result will usually
be within the range of what is possible from the employer's
point of view. There have even been cases in which the union
has bailed out a failing employer by lending him money from
the union treasury, or even, in rare cases, by agreeing to a cut
in wages to safeguard the competitive position of the company.

The modern employer, in turn, has learned to look at
things from the employee's angle. He often has an expert or
staff of experts whose entire job is understanding labor relations. There are a number of schools growing up in this
country where the men who are going to represent labor and
management study side by side, to get a common background
from which to approach their mutual problems. This modern
employer knows that prosperity cannot be attained in a mass-
production economy unless there is a mass market, and that
the purchasing power of the mass market depends almost
entirely on the purchasing power of workers. This means that
good wages are good business, and also that purchasing

power must be systematically maintained in times of income interruption due to unemployment, old age, death of the breadwinner or disability.

All this is not meant to suggest that we are reaching a point where employers and employees need not and should not have labor disputes and strikes and picketing and all-night arguments. This contest, in the nature of a free enterprise system, must be accepted. But it is, so to speak, a limited kind of warfare; it is not Total War. Back in the Middle Ages, the many petty princes throughout Europe were engaged in constant wars with each other. But each one instinctively remembered that, lurking just across the Bosporus or the Strait of Gibraltar were the Turk and the Moor. And so they never allowed their warfare to reach the point where they destroyed or unduly weakened each other, for they knew that if they did the hordes from the East would engulf them all. So here: the struggle is limited, because both sides realize that to destroy each other would be to destroy the structure of Western private enterprise and democracy—and we too would be engulfed by economic collapse and a new kind of flood from the East.

Of course there is a conflict of interest—a surface contest—between proprietors and workers over the price of the worker's services. There is also a conflict of interest between the housewife and the butcher over the price of hamburger, and between the manufacturer and the dealer over the wholesale price of air conditioners, and between a public utility and a coal supplier over the price of fuel. Yet in the endless welter of millions of hagglings and bargainings and holdouts and compromises that make up every day's business up and down our land, no one suggests that there is a class struggle between each set of bargainers. No more is it so in labor negotiations. For just as bargainers in the course of

commerce tacitly accept the fact that the lively and profit-
able trade which is the end product of the process is in everyone's interest, so labor and management realize that their
ultimate fortunes are intimately linked in the profitability
and success of the particular employing enterprise and the
general success of private enterprise everywhere.

Since the Class Struggle is a lie, even a partial acceptance
of its poisonous teaching is dangerous and should be recognized for what it is wherever it appears. Resort to violence
in labor disputes, on either side; destruction of plant or
property; studied violation of laws designed to forestall disorder; attempts to discredit a respectable employer or union
to gain an advantage; and attempts to instill and arouse
class hatreds in the course of a dispute—all these are in some
degree derivative from the Marxian doctrine, even though
the participants might indignantly deny any kinship with
Marx. These practices, fortunately rare nowadays, are to be
combated not by equally violent means, but by a policy of
carrying to complete acceptance the now-prevalent doctrine
of the essential mutuality of interest of labor, management
and the public.

The New Republican Labor Tradition

The New Republican labor tradition goes back to Abraham
Lincoln.

In 1860 Lincoln was campaigning before the Republican
convention, and he came to New Haven, where a strike of
shoemakers was in progress. The Democrats were bitterly
complaining that Republican agitators had started the strike!
Lincoln simply said:

I am glad to see that a system of labor prevails in New England
under which laborers can strike when they want to, where they
are not obliged to work under all circumstances, and are not tied

down and obliged to labor whether you pay them or not! I like the system which lets a man quit when he wants to, and wish it might prevail everywhere.

In Lincoln's ringing lines you may find the beginnings of modern American labor philosophy, and you will see the heart of the doctrines which have been set forth in this chapter.

In a world being set on fire by the Communist Manifesto's Class Struggle doctrine, Lincoln said:

There is no permanent class of hired laborers among us. Twenty-five years ago I was a hired laborer. The hired laborer of yesterday labors on his own account today, and will hire others to labor for him tomorrow. Advancement—improvement in condition—is the order of things in a society of equals.

But, in this society of equals, while everyone started even, the result was not to be egalitarian.

What is the true condition of the laborer? I take it that it is best for all to leave each man free to acquire property as fast as he can. Some will get wealthy. I don't believe in a law to prevent a man from getting rich; it would do more harm than good. So while we do not propose any war upon capital, we do wish to allow the humblest man an equal chance to get rich with everybody else. When one starts poor, as most do in the race of life, free society is such that he knows he can better his condition; he knows that there is no fixed condition of labor for his whole life.

Addressing a Workingmen's Association, Lincoln said:

"The strongest bond of human sympathy outside of the family relation should be one uniting all working people of all nations, and tongues, and kindreds."

And finally, these well-known words from President Lincoln's first annual message to Congress in 1861 elevated labor to the dignity which is the hallmark of American labor philosophy: "Labor is prior to, and independent of, capital. Capital is only the fruit of labor, and could never have existed if labor had not first existed."

Let us be clear, then, that no party has a monopoly on a tradition favorable to labor. More than a quarter of a century after Lincoln, Grover Cleveland, a Democratic President, was arresting union leaders and using troops to break a strike of the American Railway Union. A half-century after Lincoln spoke those moving words about the bond between working men, a Democratic President, Woodrow Wilson, declared himself to be "a fierce partisan of the Open Shop."

There have been leaders in both parties who were unfriendly to labor during part or all of their careers. Even in the case of Franklin Delano Roosevelt, William Green in 1935 threatened that the entire labor movement would oppose Mr. Roosevelt, and the *New York Times*, February 3, 1935, reported that labor unions had broken with the New Deal and that union leaders were "almost in despair of making headway toward union recognition in the face of powerful industrial interests and an unsympathetic administration."

President Truman, in 1945, demanded a bill to conscript labor which was vigorously opposed by unions and defeated in Congress by an opposition led by Republicans. In 1946 President Truman called for the enactment of an unprecedented strike-breaking law, giving the President power to draft strikers into the Army. Over the objections of labor, the bill passed the Democratically controlled House, but it was killed in the Senate, with every Republican Senator voting against it.

A large proportion of the really significant and pioneering accomplishments in labor law were Republican achievements. The eight-hour day was first established in 1868 by a Republican President and Congress. Republicans set up the first Bureau of Labor. Republicans raised it to Cabinet rank and made it the present Department of Labor. Republicans also created the Department of Health, Education, and Welfare.

As far back as 1896, Republicans in their party platform called for a federal law which would guarantee the right to join unions and bargain collectively. A Republican Administration in 1898 enacted legislation to forbid the firing of railroad employees for union membership. In a Republican Administration the first workmen's compensation law for government employees was passed, and it was Republican states that pioneered in workmen's compensation, child labor laws and old-age assistance.

The Republican Railway Labor Act of 1926 is still working. Republicans prohibited competition of prison labor with free labor. The Davis-Bacon Act, requiring payment of prevailing wage rates on government construction contracts, is a Republican enactment.

The Norris-LaGuardia Act of 1932, which by prohibiting labor injunctions and effectively removing the threat of anti-trust weapons against union activity set the stage for labor's great gains thereafter, was enacted by Republicans.

These facts—many of them perhaps forgotten—will serve to restore a better balance in the conception of the relation of the major parties to labor, and to remind us that the labor philosophy of the Eisenhower Administration as described in this chapter is no sudden departure; it is the direct product of a long tradition.

5

The Government and People

The final test of a political philosophy is this: what responsibility does it assign to the government for the well-being of people—not people as workers or people as businessmen or people as farmers, but people as people?

It used to be thought that political philosophies on this issue were divided into two. The one philosophy, as expressed by Grover Cleveland, held that there was no such responsibility, and that any relaxation of this view "encourages the expectations of paternal care on the part of the government and weakens the sturdiness of our national character." The other philosophy, exemplified by Communism and Socialism, purported to make the guaranteeing of mass welfare a major government function at all costs.

But there is a third and newer philosophy, which is neither *laissez faire* nor mass welfare. This view holds that the government does have some responsibility, but it is to individual persons and not to people in the mass, and it is derived from the risks inherent in a competitive free enterprise society. Moreover, this third philosophy is based, not on collectivistic or paternalistic concepts, but on typically American traditions of the worth of the individual person, the dictates of religion and rights of persons before the law.

The difference is one of motivation. If your objective is a sort of collectivized welfare—the idea that social security, public health and assured income in time of adversity are good things for society as a whole, for men in the mass and for the state itself—you will quite possibly produce an imposing array of social benefits, but with very little vestige of individual rights remaining. But if your motivation springs from a deeper sense of the value of the individual person— the idea that impoverished disability, helpless unemployment and destitute old age cripple the human personality and affront the dignity of the human spirit—then you will ultimately work out a system in which you will have the benefits of security, and, far from destroying the individual's character, you will liberate and enrich it.

There is another difference in motivation: the Socialist or Communist wants to get rid of the risk element inherent in competitive private enterprise by getting rid of private enterprise itself; we want to preserve an economy of risks, rewards and competition, and we therefore believe the government should help people secure themselves against the consequences of the risk system we want to maintain.

Both the Socialist and the *laissez-faire* philosophies are out of date. The Socialists took a look at the European economic scene a hundred years ago and concluded that the risks and the suffering of the workers could never be eliminated within the private enterprise framework, and that therefore the welfare of an entire class had to be underwritten by the drastic measure of state ownership of the means of production. The rugged individualists took a look at the American economic scene a hundred years ago, and concluded that any hard-working, honest, sober, thrifty man could make his fortune and save against a rainy day, and if for some reason he ran into trouble, his family or relatives or—as a last resort—his community could take care of him.

The Socialist theory was the product of unbridled capitalism superimposed on a stratified class system. The *laissez-faire* theory flourished under an agrarian culture based heavily on family labor and family self-sufficiency.

Anyone who has read his papers since the death of Queen Victoria knows that neither picture fits the facts of today.

In an agrarian economy, the basis of security was land, not cash wages. We are constantly being reminded of the self-reliance of those sturdy pioneers who settled the West. Yet the source of their security was the most grandiose government giveaway in history—the Homestead Act. They were not ashamed to acknowledge this, as they sang their favorite song:

> But I'm happy as a clam
> On the land of Uncle Sam,
> In my little old sod shanty on the claim.

Someone might argue that this is not the same as getting a social security check, for the homesteaders had to work to get something out of their grant. But—and here is the key to the whole business—the modern worker also has to work to get his social security, and, in a mature system, will on the average get out of it only what he puts into it, since the system is designed to be self-sustaining.

What are today's facts? Two-thirds of us live in large cities. Only about a tenth of us are farmers or farm workers. About 95 per cent of all personal income is nonagricultural. About three-fourths of all personal income is wages and salaries.

Plainly, we no longer have an agrarian economy. We have a cash-wage economy. Almost everyone depends for his daily bread on cash payments made to him every week or two by someone else.

This change requires a profound change in the attitude of government toward people.

In an agrarian society, with self-sufficient family farms and closely knit communities, there was always a place on the farm or in the old family house for the old folks, or the unemployed or disabled family member.

But in an urban society, with high standards of living, and high rents and food and clothing and medical costs, what is the man with a family supposed to do when the cash wages on which he is dependent for all these necessities are suddenly cut off, through injury, unemployment and the like?

We insist that our economy must retain its elements of competition and risk. We also know that competition and risk inevitably will leave victims of risk—victims through no fault of their own. It follows, then, that the price we must pay in modern times for the advantages of a risk economy is the assumption of responsibility by the government as well as by industry for reducing the hardships incident to those risks without damage to the inherent principles and drives of free enterprise.

Can this be done?

It can, through the modern mechanism of income insurance.

Income Insurance

Income insurance is a convenient general term for all those public systems which are designed to replace a portion of lost earnings when wages are interrupted or stopped due to old age, death, unemployment or disability. It thus includes old-age and survivors' insurance, unemployment insurance, workmen's compensation, and sickness and disability insurance.

Small sums are paid in regularly, based on the wages of the employee, so that when the wage-stopping event occurs, a fund will be available to pay some income during the wageless period. These small payments, whether social security taxes or workmen's compensation premium payments, become a predictable cost of doing business, find their way into the price of the product, and are ultimately paid for by the consumers of the product. No one has ever shown that this cost has been an impediment to private enterprise or a drag upon incentive.

The contribution of the New Republicanism in the field of income insurance has been to improve and perfect it, not as an antidepression measure, but as a regular part of our system even in times of high prosperity. The Eisenhower Administration has brought about or stimulated the greatest round of improvements in income insurance legislation, state and federal, in over fifteen years.

The Social Security amendments of 1954, proposed by the Eisenhower Administration and enacted by a Republican Congress, are interesting not only because of the fact that they improved social security, but also because of the *way* in which they did it. The striking thing about these amendments is the amount of trouble they went to in order to work individual equity in dozens of different combinations of circumstances. Here again we see the concern for individual rights and needs. There are some who would cut through all these complications and put in some kind of uniform or arbitrary benefit. But instead we keep millions of wage records, make millions of intricate calculations, and disentangle the personal work history of millions of persons over entire lifetimes, in order to retain the character of our system as one built on individual rights. Among the improvements in the 1954 amendments were the following:

Benefits were given the biggest increase in history—especially when compared with the corresponding change in cost of living.

Ten million more people were given coverage, thus making the act almost universal.

The most humane improvement in the history of the system was made in the form of a so-called disability freeze. For almost twenty years, the law had been allowed to remain in such a state that a man who became totally and permanently disabled would eventually forfeit all or most of his rights, and his past contributions as well. The 1954 amendments provided that all his rights should be preserved as of the time when he became disabled.

The disincentive effect of the earnings test after retirement was reduced, by permitting up to twelve hundred dollars a year to be earned without any loss of old-age benefits, so that earnings in a year could be bunched in a particular season or spread around, according to the individual's needs and opportunities. Previously he lost a month's benefits for any month in which he earned seventy-five dollars. The age at which he could earn an unlimited amount without loss of benefits was reduced from seventy-five to seventy-two.

A number of individualized provisions were inserted, too detailed to be described here. For example, certain widows of men who died before 1950 and who were unable to qualify under the stricter earlier rules were retroactively made eligible. The point to be noted is that this concern for people with special problems, like the disabled, or the retired people who need supplementary income, or a small neglected number of widows, is evidence of a philosophy of individualized rather than mass social security.

Unemployment insurance, for some odd reason, had never been extended by federal action before the Eisenhower Administration took office. The Republican Congress in 1954 passed President Eisenhower's bill to extend coverage to four million more employees.

The Railroad Retirement Act was liberalized in a number of ways, through increased benefits, reduction of the qualifying age for widows from sixty-five to sixty years, and co-ordination of the act with social security.

The unprecedented burst of state legislation following the messages of President Eisenhower and Secretary of Labor James P. Mitchell urging improvements has already been noted, with forty-five states improving their unemployment insurance and workmen's compensation laws.

In addition, improvements in practically all the income insurances applicable to federal employees and employees in the District of Columbia were undertaken.

Finally, the Eisenhower Administration set out to do something about the last remaining frontier of income insurance: nonoccupational sickness and disability. Most workers are protected by workmen's compensation if injured at work, but in only four states—New York, New Jersey, California and Rhode Island—is anything paid for illness or injury occurring off the job, although the loss of income is just as real. An Eisenhower Administration bill was introduced in the first session of the 84th Congress to make a start by installing a system of cash benefits in the District of Columbia for sickness and disability.

Our question in this chapter is what the New Republicanism believes about the government's responsibility for the needs of people. There has never been a period since the establishment of these systems when so much was done for the people through income insurance at both federal and state levels. This is, after all, the way in which a large part of the government's duty toward people is nowadays discharged, for it is the way in which the government deals with the exigencies which account for most of the individual person's economic emergencies. A government which does this job well has proved, more effectively than it could in any other way, that it is devoted to the well-being of people as people.

Defense Against Disaster

A second area in which a government's concern for the people is put to the test is that of the suffering caused by natural disasters such as flood, drought and hurricanes.

Something new has been happening here too. We are beginning to learn how to use the resources of Defense Mobilization to deal with destruction caused, not by enemy action, but by natural hazards.

Of course, there is nothing new in finding that the Corps of Engineers is in the midst of any flood emergency, building temporary bridges, rescuing the stranded, sandbagging the river banks.

But when the New England floods struck, something happened that had never happened before: the emergency training that had been carried out some months before in Operation Alert, under conditions of simulated bombing, was put to work to deal with the flood, without anyone's thinking there was anything remarkable about it. The Employment Service offices, which had carried through an exercise in offering their offices and services to the local Civil Defense Director, went through the same process when the flood struck, and immediately went to work around the clock furnishing needed emergency workers. The Civil Defense organization smoothly assumed charge, and practically every agency of government was soon contributing everything it had that could alleviate the hardships of the flood. Small Business Administration offered loans; the Public Health Service looked after water and contagion problems; the Department of Agriculture worked on the food problem; the Department of Commerce went to work on getting the industries re-established; the Department of Labor's state-federal Employment Security system stepped up unemployment insurance procedures and conducted emergency job placements.

Most interesting of all, however, was the way in which Defense Mobilization measures were used. In order to get some of the plants on their feet again, the Office of Defense Mobilization opened some of its "expansion goals" for certain products for the specific benefit of these plants, so that orders could be placed with them and aid given them in getting re-established.

In addition, President Eisenhower has asked for legislation under which the federal government would provide some kind of disaster insurance to fill the need which private insurance has been unable to fill.

Earlier in the book there was also some mention of the series of positive actions taken to alleviate the effects of the drought in Texas—including Public Law 875, the President's Disaster Relief Fund, the feed program for basic herds, the system of transporting hay from further north and the livestock loan program.

Both the concern and the effectiveness of the government in time of suffering due to natural catastrophe have risen to new heights, in line with what most people have come to expect of their government.

Aid Without Control

The distinctive thing about many looming political issues of the future is they involve traditionally local matters which have become so pressing that their very severity has made them a subject for federal concern. Among these matters are: roads, housing, hospitals, health, schools and safety.

These are diverse problems, but one thing they have in common: they demand that the federal government provide money, and at the same time scrupulously abstain from control. There is widespread insistence that the federal government embark on a generous program of aid to education, but no one would be so foolhardy as to suggest that the federal government should control educational policy in even the slightest degree.

This poses a challenge of some difficulty and delicacy.

Let us set down in the simplest possible terms a general agreement on what a federal policy for the future should contain, if it is to meet this swiftly growing problem of the relation of the central government to local needs.

1. The federal government must act, and act vigorously. It is no good at this point to speculate about what the states should or should not have done, or whose fault it is that we find ourselves in our present posture. The plain fact is that we are short of classrooms, short of roads, short of medical facilities and research, and short of what could be accomplished in industrial safety, housing, water supply and other needs of the people. The problem will not be solved by saying over and over again that the states and local communities should have done something about this long ago. Actually, a considerable part of the cause is the interruption of normal development due to the war, coupled with an increase in population which seems to have taken everyone by surprise.

2. The federal government is the only entity that has the authority and resources to set in motion a solution to this problem that will be both adequate and prompt. It can combine technical assistance, stimulation of simultaneous state action, and partial provision of needed financing, throughout the entire area of need. No one else can.

3. States should as far as possible remain the operating agencies, and the federal government should withhold its hand from active control. There are many reasons for this, some of which have been discussed in the chapter on state-federal balance. Our country is too vast, and our communities too various, to permit centrally directed policy on education or most of these other matters.

4. The policy should be so worked out that its effect is to strengthen rather than weaken state responsibility and capacity. At this point there is a noticeable cleavage between New Republicanism and its Opposition.

There are two ways you can go at this job. One is to assume that the federal government must inevitably take over more and more of the financing of such things as education and health and roads. The other is to use the federal program to build up the states more and more with a view to making them ultimately as self-sustaining as possible. As has been shown in the chapter on federal-state relations, the state governments have recently given evidence of their increasing willingness and ability to assume added responsibilities of this kind.

Anyone who puts forward a set of proposals in this area ought to be prepared to announce which of these two approaches he really believes in. The Opposition has never made its stand clear, but it is a fair assumption, from its past history of mistrust of state governments, that it regards increasing federal participation as inevitable.

The New Republican position is plain. Recognizing that federal participation on a large scale is now necessary in some of these departments, it aims ultimately toward such improved fiscal posture in the states that the effect of the over-all effort will have been to build up rather than weaken the states.

School construction is a good concrete example with which to illustrate these points of policy.

The Eisenhower Administration's approach to the matter of needed schoolrooms is quite simple.

First: what is the shortage?

The answer seems to be: about 470,000 classrooms. Of course, this is a flexible and debatable figure, for it includes not only outright shortages, but a large allowance for obsolescent classrooms. What is or is not obsolescent is a matter that cannot be reduced to provable statistics, and the matter is further complicated by the fact that the shifts in population have in many places produced shortages, not in the absolute sense, but in the sense that the schools are not in the right places. But the figure of 470,000 is probably as good a working figure as can be arrived at.

Second: what progress is now being made to reduce this backlog?

State and local expenditures of about two billion dollars a year are just about keeping even with the need for new classrooms, and adding perhaps five thousand classrooms a year. It is evident that, at this rate, the time required to wipe out our classroom deficit would be far too long to be tolerated.

Third: what would it cost to get rid of this schoolroom deficit in some reasonable period—say, five years?

To make this calculation, first assume that the states and

localities will go on increasing their rate of construction as they have in the recent past.

Then figure the amount above this that would be needed to complete our classroom supply in five years, allowing for increased school population in the meantime.

Finally, take half of this figure as the federal matching share.

On this kind of calculation, the federal expenditure becomes $250 million a year for five years, to be matched in new expenditures (above those that would be undertaken anyway) by the states and localities.

This would do the job of bringing our school facilities up to the point of adequacy.

But note several important features bearing on federal-state responsibilities.

One is the underlying assumption that states will continue to increase their exertions at the present rate in any event. Nothing would be gained if, to the extent federal money became available, state and local financing to the same extent began to dry up.

Again, the requirement of local matching of the new federal money is inherent in the plan. In the process of working up this matching money, the fiscal competence of the states will inevitably be permanently strengthened through the finding of new sources of revenue.

Most important of all, the plan is so constructed that it theoretically has an end. The idea is that this five-year burst of building will knock out the deficit, and that thereafter current needs can be met without emergency measures. Whether this will work out in practice is a question. But the intention is there, and to the extent it is realized we will be spared the prospect of a permanent and perhaps increasing loss of a traditionally local responsibility. It is better to try to work it out this way than to set out in advance with the deliberate expectation of increasing federalization of education into the indefinite future.

It should be noted also that this plan is so devised that federal interference in educational policy is avoided. The financing participation is confined to outright construction. As a matter of common sense, helping to build a building cannot involve much control of education. The building is built; the federal government goes away and has no more to do with it. If, on the other hand, the demands of the opposition for federal continuing aid for school maintenance are heeded, there is an increase in the risk of control. For now the federal government would be involved on a day-by-day basis. The continuance of everyday educational activity gradually becomes dependent on federal money. Can anyone doubt that the possession of this grip upon educational financing would eventually lead to some assertion of control? If the federal authorities think their funds are being squandered, or perhaps being used to teach questionable doctrines, will they merely look the other way and continue blindly to hand out maintenance money without question?

It is better not to run such a risk. By concentrating on construction, the federal government can make a contribution and still avoid even the suspicion of control.

The question may be raised: how is all this to be defended as a federal government activity?

There are several arguments that have been offered in justification of federal aid to education.

Our underlying philosophy, it will be recalled, is this: if a job has to be done to meet the needs of people, and no one else can do it, then it is a proper function of the federal government. The immediate job is the emergency task of eliminating our classroom shortage. It will not be done if the federal government does not help. If it is not done, the result will be that thousands of our children will be deprived of the kind of education they are entitled to. That is reason enough for federal action.

Another argument is that we must have better basic education in the interests of national defense. To take only one illustration: in one large area of the country, it has been found that almost one out of four persons cannot pass the simple fourth grade test which the Armed Forces give as a minimum requirement. One out of every two from this region falls into the Armed Forces' Group IV or below, which means that they are not material for any further training.

Here is a large segment of our population which, for want of proper education, is missing an opportunity to contribute not only to defense but also to the needs of the civilian economy for trained skilled manpower. It can well be argued that this is a legitimate matter for federal concern.

Another good example of how to meet the needs of people while avoiding excessive federal control is the Eisenhower Administration's proposed Grant-in-Aid for Industrial Safety Bill.

There are almost two million work injuries every year, and about fourteen thousand industrial deaths. The man-days lost, as President Eisenhower pointed out to the President's Conference on Occupational Safety in 1954, would build a million six-room houses.

The tragic thing about this record is that most of these injuries and deaths are preventable. This assertion is not mere rhetoric; it is demonstrable fact. Safety campaigns sponsored by the Department of Labor, using modern techniques and trained men, have reduced the accident frequency rate in high-accident industries dramatically; for example, North Carolina reduced accidents in its laundry business by

79 per cent and in its fertilizer industry by 47.3 per cent. One federal agency cut its accidents to one-sixth of what they had been.

Here again, the operating responsibility is mostly in the hands of the states, and, of course, of private employers, unions and associations. The federal government sponsors safety programs, trains safety personnel, studies hazards and issues bulletins on safety measures, draws safety codes and gets their adoption by agreement, and actually enforces safety rules in certain areas such as mines and railroads. But the direct governmental responsibility for industrial safety is in the state safety program.

Here we find a story of tragic neglect in some states. Half of the states spend less than one thin dime per year per worker on industrial safety. Five do not have a single full-time safety inspector. Thirteen states have less than five safety inspectors for the entire state. This does not involve only the less industrialized states. One state, for example, has 122,000 industrial establishments with 1,300,000 workers —and two part-time safety inspectors!

Not long ago, a Department of Labor employee visiting a plant on matters unconnected with safety noticed that there were electrical wires lying around on a very wet floor. He immediately reported this condition to the state safety authorities. They said they would look into it as soon as they could spare an inspector when he might be in that part of the state. Months went by; no inspector was available; and the inevitable happened. A man was electrocuted.

A man is dead because a state would not spend the cost of a package of cigarettes per year on his safety.

In 1954 the Eisenhower Administration drew up and urged passage of a bill under which the federal government would provide grants to any state which would install a modern safety department and share in the financing of it. It did not obtain a hearing in the first session of the 84th Congress.

Once again—as in the other federal-state ventures—the net result of this kind of system will not be the aggrandizement of power to the federal government at the expense of the states. On the contrary, when the system has worked itself out, there will be a strong state safety program where no such program existed before.

This is the universal story of similar federal-state systems, such as public health, according to the official findings of the Committee on Intergovernmental Relations. The state gains administrative strength by actually operating the system; it gains fiscal strength by raising its matching funds; it gains prestige and stature by doing another important job well.

The Unemployment Problem, Modern Version

"What is the use of living in an Empire on which the sun never sets, if one must live out one's life in an alley into which the sun never shines?"

This cry out of the past, from some forgotten Englishman, contains a thought which we must never lose sight of in our days of prosperity.

While employment is at an all-time high, and unemployment is relatively low, this is small comfort to the man or woman who, for some reason, is still unemployed. It has been shown earlier that there is an important difference between unemployment-because-of-depression and unemployment-in-spite-of-prosperity. If remedies designed for the former are applied to the latter, the final result may be more unemployment than ever. The kind of unemployment we have now is mostly either in particular areas with special problems, or among particular groups of people having special employment disadvantages, such as older workers.

The Eisenhower Administration announced in October, 1955, a specific program to reduce chronic unemployment in persistent-labor-surplus areas. The significant thing about this project is that it is carefully tailored to the kind of unemployment involved. It is not a sweeping WPA or relief activity; it is not a multibillion-dollar pump-priming venture; it is not an attempt to release billions of dollars of extra purchasing power generally; in short, it is not a New Deal anti-depression affair. Rather, it goes straight to the local problem and attempts to deal with it.

First, it co-ordinates both existing and projected exertions into a concentrated attack on the problem in any given community. There are already available, for example, the following devices and activities:

1. Department of Commerce Area Development Division, which gives technical assistance to communities on industrial redevelopment.
2. Department of Labor Community Development Program, analyzing skill and manpower resources of communities, making interstate referrals from surplus to shortage areas, aiding in planning training or retraining to meet new industrial needs and so on.
3. Manpower Policy No. 4, under which defense procurement preference is given on a certain set-aside portion of defense contracts to labor surplus areas.
4. The tax amortization plan, under which fast tax write-offs are given to plants which locate in labor surplus areas.
5. The Buy-American exception, under which goods to be produced in labor surplus areas may be given preference in procurement over foreign goods for which the bid is lower.

6. Small Business Administration loans.
7. Urban Renewal, under which a large appropriation is available for extensive improvement of blighted areas—which may be an important factor in attracting new business to labor surplus areas.

All these activities and others are in progress; the projected plan will serve to bring them all to bear effectively on a specific community plan.

The second feature of the chronic unemployment area proposal is the provision of technical assistance, both directly and through grants, to the community and its private and local agencies working on its redevelopment. This involves hard-headed analysis of the peculiar impediments that are blocking the community's prosperity—and the impediments may be quite different from one city to the next. Perhaps it is a transportation difficulty; perhaps water, or utilities, or smoke; in some instances it may be unattractive residential areas, lack of recreational or parking or hospital or educational facilities; maybe it is a labor relations history, or a lack of diversification in products, or shortcomings in management, or lack of trained skills of a usable kind among men who have spent their working lives in a single industry which now cannot give them work. In most cases there will probably be a combination of several of these.

The state and local people, working with the federal agency, will work out the nature of the difficulty and contrive an over-all plan for the community.

The third part of the project is the provision of the necessary capital to get the plan into effect. Some of it may come from existing sources, such as Small Business or Urban Renewal. In addition, a new federal lending authority is to be available, which will supply part of the capital needed. The idea, however, is that the greater part of the capital must come from the private enterprisers, and a substantial part from the state. Thus, only if a workable plan is drawn, and only if state and local interests have demonstrated their faith in it by putting their money on it, will the federal funds be forthcoming.

This, then, is a current mechanism geared to the current version of the unemployment problem.

Other parts of the Eisenhower Administration's approach to the unemployment question show the same realization of the specialized character of the need. For example, a full-scale drive to reduce unjustified discrimination against mature workers on grounds solely of age was launched in 1955 by the Labor Department. An authoritative answer to the question whether mature workers (forty-five and over—which is where discrimination begins to be noticed) are in fact as good workers as others is being sought through an extensive analysis of productivity, performance, absenteeism, injury experience and general rating on the job. The solution to the problem of alleged added cost of pension coverage, often cited as a reason why employers cannot afford to hire mature workers, is being worked on by a panel of experts. Successful employer plans for dealing with the matter in individual business are being assembled and analyzed and shown to other employers. Union contract provisions attempting to deal with age problems are being appraised for their value in reducing discrimination. Counseling of older workers, specialized placement activities and techniques to adapt workers to jobs and jobs to workers are being stepped up. Special campaigns are in progress to utilize mature women, with necessary retraining or refresher courses, in meeting such shortages as those for teachers, nurses and stenographers.

In such ways the Eisenhower Administration has approached the contemporary brand of unemployment. These moves may be unspectacular, but they are relevant to today's needs, and that is the important thing. We have general prosperity; the job now is to make that prosperity reach to special areas and special groups of people who, for various reasons, have not participated as they should in the blessings of these good times. This is important not only for the happiness of the people affected; it is important also because the well-being of these areas and groups will in turn be reflected in the productivity and wealth and happiness of the whole country.

6

Is It Conservatism?

What is conservatism?

There is good conservatism and bad conservatism. Or, if you like, there is true conservatism and false conservatism.

The difference depends on what you set out to conserve.

And this difference is the difference between ends and means.

True conservatism aims to preserve and foster the great ultimate ideals and values of our country and civilization, utilizing in any era the mechanisms that will best serve that purpose, and changing and adapting these mechanisms to the times whenever necessary to accomplish the main object.

False conservatism guards and cherishes the mechanisms of the past, and abhors new mechanisms, while ignoring in the meantime what happens to our traditional ideals and values. It worships the shell of the past, and lets the living substance die.

President Eisenhower, in his speech of September 21, 1953, at the Boston Garden, said:

The supreme belief of our society is the dignity and freedom of the individual. . . .

This supreme ideal—not merely the votes of so many Congressmen or Senators—is what sends aid to drought-stricken areas, guarantees an income to farmers, banishes needless restrictions on private enterprise, guards the free union of workers, extends the protection of social insurance to the aged and to the needy. . . .

In this, we proclaim nothing very new.

"Nothing very new?" cries the old-fashioned conservative. "Nothing very new?"—social insurance, guarding unions, farm price supports, federal aid to drought areas! Not one of these things had even been dreamed of in this country seventy-five years ago!

The answer is easy. It is the "supreme belief" that is old, as old as our oldest traditions; what is new is the machinery to give effect to the old ideals in a changing society.

If grandma is seen driving down the street in an Aston-Martin sports car with dual exhausts, we do not shake our heads over grandma—if we know she is really on her way to church. But if grandma is riding in a horse-drawn surrey, all bundled up with veils and robes—and if she is on her way to the gambling casino for a few hands of blackjack— then we have good cause to worry about grandma. It is, in short, not the vehicle that determines whether grandma is sound or suspect—it is the destination.

What are the ideals that we think of as having made our country distinctive and great? Among them are:

1. The religious conviction of the *dignity*—even divinity— of man.
2. The all-pervading ideal of *freedom*.
3. The *economic* idea that self-reliance and *initiative* of free men in a setting of private property and enterprise are the mainsprings of prosperity.
4. The *legal* concept of *equality* of opportunity and equality before the law.

5. The *cultural* idea of *individuality*—the right to be treated as a unique person.
6. The *human* right to the pursuit of happiness.
7. The *political* idea of the ultimate *sovereignty* of the individual person.

It may be noted that this catalogue reads like a checklist of all the things totalitarianism is not. For every entry on the list, there is a corresponding entry in the totalitarian credo as exemplified by the Soviet brand of Communism, which reads just the opposite.

1. The individual is insignificant and expendable and should have pride only in the State, and as for divinity—since there is no Divinity above, you cannot very well look for it here below.
2. There is no freedom, but complete subjection to the State.
3. The mainspring of progress is the desire to enhance the greatness of the State.
4. Opportunity is controlled by the State; the law is an instrument to achieve the objectives of the State.
5. The person is not an individual, but a unit of production and consumption.
6. Happiness is irrelevant, although promotion of some degree of contentment may be necessary to prevent disorder and increase production.
7. There is no political sovereignty in the individual; power lies in the State, in the Party, and especially in the heads of the Party.

Never before have the lines been so clearly drawn between two sets of beliefs contending for the minds of men. Never before has it been so important that we know what we are trying to conserve, and that we do not make the mistake of consuming our energies defending musty mechanisms while the ideals themselves are forgotten in the skirmishing.

Let us try this distinction between ultimate ideals and mechanisms on an example. There is no better litmus paper with which to judge the nature of a political philosophy than social insurance. Many "conservatives" assume that they must automatically be hostile to such things as social security, unemployment insurance and workmen's compensation. They realize, of course, that when a man's income is destroyed because of injury or unemployment you cannot let him and his family starve—but, if pressed, they will usually say that the best way to handle such matters is public relief.

Now, relief is by far the older mechanism; it dates from the Poor Laws of the first Queen Elizabeth of England. Social security in this country is younger than the present Queen Elizabeth.

But which of the two best serves the ideals we have just listed?

Dignity? The whole idea of income insurance was to get away from the humiliation that attends public relief and to provide insured benefits as of right that can be collected without apology to anyone.

Freedom? The relief recipient loses his freedom to keep his financial affairs to himself, his freedom to move where he pleases, his freedom to spend his money as he likes. The social security beneficiary can go where he pleases, spend his money on anything he likes, and no one can call him to account.

Incentive? No amount of past effort will increase your rights to relief; but the more you work and earn, the larger (within limits) your social security rights are apt to be.

Equality? The relief recipient still is apt to feel like a second-class citizen; the social security beneficiary exercises rights common to practically all other working persons, including bank presidents.

Individuality? Relief assigns a uniform subsistence level; social security rights are based on individual wage records.

Happiness? Well, happiness is an elusive thing; but the man who knows, all his life, that he has a set of social insurances against the major exigencies of life has a much better chance to pursue happiness than the man who is tortured by fear of what would happen to him and his family if he were injured, killed, retired or fired.

Sovereignty? On relief, the individual takes what he gets; under income insurance, he not only builds up his own rights, but has a voice in determining in advance what they will be.

What it comes down to is this: your false conservative believes in freedom, dignity and equality of the individual person—until that person gets sick or loses his job or is retired as overage and finds himself without income; after that, his dignity and equality and freedom can go hang.

There is nothing new about this fallacy of false conservatism; it has existed in all ages. It is not so long ago that universal free public education was viewed as radical by false conservatives—yet education serves every one of our deepest ideals. Was the Homestead Act a subversive move, just because it was the biggest giveaway in history? Was President Lincoln a Bolshevik because he uttered the Emancipation Proclamation? Was President Washington's Secretary of the Treasury Alexander Hamilton a Red because he founded the Bank of the United States? All these things were novel devices—more drastic departures at the time than, say, the Soil Bank or grants-in-aid for school construction are now. But we do not consider them alien to our traditions, because they all contributed directly and obviously toward the conservation of our best ideals of the value of the individual person.

Travelers to England used to be perplexed to see two gorgeously uniformed guards marching up and down in front of an old building in London. The building seemed to have no particular reason for being so honored. Upon inquiry, the travelers would be told the real explanation. The Bank of England used to be housed in that building years before. Then, one day, they moved the bank to a new location. But somehow no one had ever told the guards to stop guarding the vacated building. So they continued their faithful guard, in their splendid uniforms, over the shell of a building from whence the treasure had long since departed.

The analogy needs no belaboring. But it may help to picture vividly the equal folly of marshaling the full panoply and armament of conservatism to stand guard over the hollow husk of some outworn device or method, while the real treasure of our traditional values has moved with the moving times, and must be guarded in other places by other means.

The American Version of Conservatism

A lot of books and articles have been written lately about conservatism, but most of them seem to miss the most obvious point of all about American conservatism.

American conservatism does not spring from the same roots as British and Continental conservatism; in fact, its roots are in *revolt* against that kind of conservatism.

One of these books begins with a tentative summary of the characteristics of conservatism. One of the hallmarks of conservatism, says this author, was belief in a permanent stratified class structure of society.

Certainly—for France or Italy or England, which look back over a history of aristocracy and feudalism, which still cling to their titles and classes, and which will tell you they can easily identify a "gentleman" just by looking at him and listening to him speak. But not so in a country whose conservatism sets out to conserve a tradition which begins with the words: "All men are created equal."

Once we hold it steadily in mind that our American conservatism conserves principles born of Revolution, not of complacency, everything will be much clearer. But that Revolution was against other wrongs beside inequality.

Everything in our history cries out against a big and domineering government, for it was against just such an overbearing central authority that the colonies rebelled.

Every page of our early story speaks eloquently of the rights of the states and of the people, and shows forth an aversion to concentration of power at any point, for it was just such a concentration of executive power that drove the Americans to revolt.

The homely maxims of hard work, equal opportunity, earning an honest reward for effort, standing on your own feet without help from the government—all these are embedded in our economic tradition as surely as individual and local responsibility are embedded in our political background.

Let us make no mistake about it then: those who would put class over class, or class against class, and those who would push us into big central government, and those who would try to suppress the right of working people to fight their way up the economic ladder, and those who want to interfere with the operation of the forces of competition, initiative and free markets—all these are not conservers. They are your true radicals. For they draw their ideas from the alien world against which our forefathers broke away in violent protest.

The Fatal Fear of Being Obvious

The bane of American political thought for many years has been an inclination to be ashamed of homespun American principles of the kind we hear orated about on the Fourth of July.

There are two directions in which people have tried to escape from this homely line of thought.

One is to go aristocratic—which means to lapse into European-type "conservatism," with its class distinctions, its clinging to privilege, and its doctrine of the natural superiority of whoever happens to be on top.

The other is to go pseudo-intellectual—which often means to take over Marxian ideas in some degree or other. Maybe not Communism—but a fondness for solving all problems through strong central executive action, a disposition to ridicule the normal operation of human and economic motivations and substitute governmental direction, and a contempt for local and state governments, businessmen, money, success, saving, hard work and all such "bourgeois claptrap."

Anyone who reached adulthood during the thirties does not need any further introduction to this second bent of mind. Among those who argued politics all night at a back table in the College Coffee Shop, who would have dared to take his stand on the simple concepts of the American tradition that we all know so well? His companions would have laughed him down. To sparkle in such settings, your thought had to have at least some exotic trappings; to be obvious was unforgivable, even if the obvious happened to be right.

The political philosophy of President Eisenhower is, in a sense, more sophisticated and advanced than that of this type of so-called intellectual. He has dared to be obvious when the obvious was right. He has dared to exalt the local product and ignore the glamour of the imported idea. He has

had both the wisdom and the courage to steer us at last out
of a twenty-year period in which much of our political
thought, especially among some university people, writers
and journalists, was essentially Europe-based, and he has
brought us back to our own traditions.

It only remains for these people to reach the same stage
of sophistication that many American artists, musicians, poets
and novelists have attained. They have managed to emanci-
pate themselves from a long history of dependence on European models and to create an indigenous product. But many
of our political writers, analysts and intellectuals are slower
in this process.

The challenge to them is even more exciting, if they would
take it. The staleness of Marxian dialectic, the tiredness of
the Socialist clichés that sounded so smart during the thirties, the utter and unquestionable wrongness of Europe-
based political dogmas when transplanted to our soil—all
these must surely soon drive the independent intellectual
to the exhilarating discovery of the primitive beauty of traditional American political and economic theory. Politics is,
in the end, a pragmatic art, and economics is a pragmatic
science. The principles of New Republicanism work. The
intellectual of the future will be the man who recognizes this
simple truth, and builds a native American system of political thought on our own facts, and experiences, and aspirations, and history, and national personality.

Still Plenty to Do

To say that a wide area of consensus has been reached and
that the extremism of the thirties is out of place is not to
conclude that the future holds nothing but dull conformity
within a placid Utopia. We need as much as ever before—
perhaps more—the crusader, the reformer, the dissenter, the
young man or woman who rebels against the world's wrongs,

the idealist who gives us visions apparently beyond our power to attain, the Jeremiahs and Savonarolas and Jeremy Benthams and Carry Nations. There are still thousands of things wrong in the world waiting to be put right—any one of which a young person could consecrate his life to and deem it well spent.

We are often told that young people nowadays do not seem to go in for the kind of violent political protest that used to be seen in the thirties. They do not go about carrying banners or staging demonstrations or writing inflammatory poetry. This has led Thornton Wilder to coin for them the name of "The Silent Generation."

Does this mean that the spark and dash have gone out of today's young people?

Decidedly not. What has happened is that all discussion now takes place under the grim shadow of weapons of destruction that can obliterate the race. Moreover, the United States is no longer on the sidelines, offering criticism, suggestions, material help and sometimes eventually military support; it is carrying the principal responsibility for peace and freedom in the world.

And so, in a very real sense, the excitement, the dangers and the struggles that confront "The Silent Generation" are such as to make the flurries of the thirties seem artificial and pale by comparison. It is the sobering effect of this increased world responsibility that accounts for the outward difference in the attitude and actions of this generation. As Thornton Wilder said,

The emerging International Man will move less feverishly in his enlarged thought-world. This generation is silent because these changes call not for argument but for rumination.

Never before has a country faced a challenge in the ideological realm comparable to ours. Our peace and even our survival may depend on our success in obtaining understanding throughout the world of our motives and ideals, and in building up the self-respect and self-determination of a bewildering variety of other countries. Note the unprecedented subtlety of the assignment. We are not setting out to convert the world to our own ideas and to remake others in our own image, as has been tried sometimes by others in the past, and as is being tried by the Communists now. Rather, we are trying in every possible way to help other countries realize their own potentials within the framework of their own cultures. To do this, while achieving genuine comprehension (not imitation) of our own culture and aspirations, by people with entirely different economic, philosophical and political backgrounds, is a task of the utmost difficulty. If we put all our best thinkers, all our best writers, all our best artists, all our best speakers, all our best labor experts, all our best dramatists and actors, all our best technical and professional people to this task, it would be none too many.

Yet this is but one example of the unfinished jobs at hand. Many more from the international field could be listed; but since the present analysis has centered round domestic matters, it might be more appropriate to suggest a few samples from the home front.

It has been pointed out that from 1953 to 1956 the happy combination of lively industrial expansion with a stabilized cost of living was achieved. The challenge for the future is the question whether we can really maintain this combination while still preserving the healthy volatility that market prices should have in a free economy. Certainly here is an opportunity to command the interest of the most brilliant economists we can produce.

We are moving into an era of accelerated technological

change and automation; can we obtain the blessings of more leisure and less drudgery and still not produce undue dislocation and unemployment? Undoubtedly we can, if with good will we apply our best talent and thought to the matter.

Can we over the long pull meet the twentieth-century demands placed upon government without dangerous centralization of power, and can we perfect state and municipal government to assume the roles they must assume in our changing, urbanized society? We can, but it will take a lot of original thinking and hard work.

Then there is the entire range of needs of people, with room for tremendous improvement in every category: education, at all levels; skills training, to meet both civilian and military needs; health, medical expense and rehabilitation; disaster relief; income loss through disability; highway improvements and safety; a continuing solution to the farm problem; the problem of school integration and racial tensions; the problem of juvenile delinquency—one could go on and on and compile a pressing agenda for the years ahead which would fill a book in itself.

The point, then, is not that our achievement of a considerable degree of balance and consensus should make us self-satisfied; rather, it should make us all the more eager to get on with the jobs still to be done, with the confidence born of a conviction that our own basic political, economic and ethical principles are demonstrably working, and that our combined abilities are demonstrably equal to the task.

7

Is It the New Deal?

The Opposition, in the intervals when they are not accusing
the Eisenhower Administration of being the slave of Big
Business, will often be heard to say that the Eisenhower
Administration is after all nothing but a continuation of the
New Deal.

In this statement they presumably intend to refer to the
accomplishments and plans of the Eisenhower Administration in social security, unemployment insurance, workmen's
compensation, disability insurance, minimum wage laws,
maximum hours legislation, disaster relief, housing, school
construction, trade union strength, labor peace, employment
conditions for federal and District of Columbia employees,
safety programs, help for special groups such as older workers and so on.

But does this make the New Republicanism an extension
of the New Deal? The answer is no.

What Was the New Deal?

The first fallacy in this comparison is the supposition that
the New Deal was a coherent political philosophy. It was
not. It was a series of trial-and-error measures, some good,
some bad—some liberal, some conservative—some warmly

humanitarian, some coldly political—some probusiness, some antibusiness—some long-range, some aimed at the expediency of the moment.

One observer remarked that Mr. Roosevelt reminded him of nothing so much as an elevator boy caught between two floors and frantically pushing all the buttons.

President Roosevelt himself characterized his approach as that of a football quarterback, who could not be expected to call the next play until he had seen how the last play had worked.

With the generous forgetfulness of time, all this has merged and mellowed in many memories into a vague association of the New Deal with "liberalism." The next step is to say that any move which is "liberal" is "New Dealish."

Professor Hofstadter, in his book *American Political Tradition*, has said that there were really two New Deals, and that even within these two New Deals there was no real thread except political improvisation.

The first New Deal centered round the National Recovery Administration. This was not a social or humanitarian or labor measure; it was a device aimed at rescuing business. And the philosophy of it could hardly be called liberal, since it was based upon keeping prices up, restricting the volume of production and permitting the kind of concerted action among businessmen that would ordinarily be barred by the antitrust laws. In fact, as soon as NRA was declared unconstitutional, businessmen who merely continued practices started under NRA were successfully prosecuted for violation of the Sherman Anti-Trust Act.

The economic philosophy announced at the outset of the New Deal, so far as there was one, was a composite of two ideas:

1. The country had reached the end of its era of expansion and entered an era in which the main job was that of controlling a more equitable distribution of the things produced.
2. The task of planning and controlling this distribution was the proper responsibility of the federal government.

These two ideas are set forth with disarming candor in Mr. Roosevelt's famous 1932 Commonwealth Club speech in San Francisco:

The turn of the tide came with the turn of the century . . . equality of opportunity as we have known it no longer exists. Our industrial plant is built; the problem just now is whether under existing conditions it is not overbuilt. Our last frontier has long since been reached. . . .

Whether the current economic philosophy is an offshoot of this New Deal idea may best be seen from a few figures (1932 figures expressed in dollars should be roughly doubled for a fair comparison):

Expenditures on industrial construction in the year in which "our industrial plant is built": $ 74 million
Expenditure on industrial construction in 1955: $2,403 million

Production in the year in which our industrial plant was suspected of being "overbuilt": | Production in 1955:

Steel: 15 million tons | 117 million tons
Aluminum: 52,000 tons | 1,565,785 tons
Power: 79 billion KWH | 546 billion KWH

Population of the West in the year in which "our last frontier has long since been reached": 12 million
Population of the West, 1955: 23 million

Mr. Roosevelt went on:

A mere builder of more industrial plants, a creator of more rail-road systems, an organizer of more corporations, is as likely to be a danger as a help. . . .

Our task now is not discovery or exploitation of natural re-sources, or necessarily producing more goods. It is the soberer, less dramatic business of administering resources and plants al-ready in hand, of seeking to re-establish foreign markets for our surplus production, of meeting the problem of underconsumption, of adjusting production to consumption, of distributing wealth and products more equitably, of adapting existing economic or-ganizations to the service of the people.

Production of natural gas in the year in which the task was no longer "exploitation of natural resources":	1½ trillion cu. ft.
Production of natural gas, 1955:	9 trillion cu. ft.
Production of oil in the year discovery was no longer our task:	65½ million bbls. per mo.
Production of oil, November, 1955:	210 million bbls. per mo.
Gross national product in the year when our task was not "producing more goods":	$58½ billion
Gross national product, 1955:	$387½ billion
Gross private investment in the year in which our task was merely "administering resources and plants already in hand":	$900 million
Gross private investment, 1955:	$59,400 million
Expenditure on personal consumption in year in which the task was to adjust production to consumption:	$49 billion
Expenditure on personal consumption, 1955:	$252½ billion

The Great Fallacy of the New Deal approach—which per-sists in some degree down to this day—is the assumption that welfare and social justice for the common man will be better promoted by concentrating on equitable distribution of the resources "already in hand" than by realizing the almost unlimited potential of this country of more resources for all. The concepts of social justice, and some of the measures adopted to further them, were good, and have indeed been carried forward under the New Republicanism. But—and here is the crucial difference—they have now been successfully blended into a philosophy which has shown that an equitable sharing of resources can be combined with an economic system which greatly increases those resources. In short, the humanitarian ideas of the New Deal were praiseworthy and have been rightly emulated; the economic ideas were bad, and have been rightly discarded.

Now we come to the role of government in all this. Mr. Roosevelt, in the same speech, went on to say:

As I see it, the task of government in its relation to business is to assist the development of an economic declaration of rights, an economic constitutional order. . . .

Happily, the times indicate that *to create such an order not only is the proper policy of Government,* but it is the *only* line of safety for our economic structures as well. [Italics supplied]

Here, then, is another New Deal dogma which is the flat contrary of the New Republicanism: *the New Deal said that it is the government's job to create an economic order.*

This economic order was designed to bring about the well-being of the common man; and yet, although Mr. Roosevelt said in the same speech that "we are now providing a drab living for our own people," this was somehow to be accomplished by beginning with the assumption that our economy was already overbuilt! This paradox jumps right out of single speech. It was a fatal flaw going to the very heart of the New Deal program.

It is clear that the New Republicanism owes nothing to

the first New Deal—the New Deal of the NRA, the overbuilt industrial plant and the economic order to be "created" by the government.

The second New Deal, in Professor Hofstadter's classification, began in 1935. Labor was threatening to oppose President Roosevelt, and was calling NRA the "National Run Around." The NRA was declared unconstitutional; the depression was still going strong, with over ten million unemployed, and there was not much left of the first New Deal. It was at about this time that there came to full fruition both President Roosevelt's alliance with labor and his break with business. A series of legislative enactments followed, some of which have survived: the Wagner Labor Relations Act; the Social Security Act; the Holding Company Act; a stiff "wealth tax"; a large new WPA; the Housing Act of 1937; the Farm Security Act; and the Fair Labor Standards Act (minimum wage law).

After NRA had been declared unconstitutional, thus freeing business from the first New Deal to some extent, there was a period of a couple of years during which a measure of recovery was accomplished. The Gross National Product for 1937, in constant dollars, overtook the 1929 figure (although well below half the 1955 figure). There were still almost eight million people unemployed, but the mature-economy overbuilt-plant school of thought became alarmed and apparently thought they had an incipient boom on their hands. And so Federal Reserve officials *tightened credit*, and spending and relief were sharply cut. Immediately the business index plunged; and President Roosevelt at that point seemed to decide once and for all that the stimulus of government spending was a necessary part of his economic policy. This conviction has remained a characteristic tenet of Opposition economics; a demand for lavish federal spending is the standard reaction of these critics now whenever there is a business downturn, just as it was in 1938. Similarly, a certain timidity about our country's potential range of prosperity is also still traceable to the days when a Gross National Product of 90 billion dollars (compared with the present 387 billion) was considered a danger signal. The spending tradition was seen to be undiminished as late as the time of the 1954 downturn; the timidity about too much prosperity reappeared at the time the 1955 upturn was in full swing.

The recession of 1938 signaled the end of the New Deal's major experimentation. There followed more spending, a burst of trust-busting, and a redoubled attack upon Big Business. But it remained for the advent of war to pull the country out of its economic trough.

If the New Deal is judged by its principal objective, which was to bring material well-being to the people, there is no escape from a bleak conclusion. It was a failure.

In all fairness, it must be said that the New Deal was attempting to cope with problems of appalling difficulty, without benefit of techniques and experience now available. It would not be fair to question in retrospect the intelligence or ability of the leaders of the period in the light of what we have learned since. But it is certainly fair to criticize those who, with full opportunity to see the failure of New Deal policies to bring prosperity, and with full opportunity to see the prosperity that has attended the success of New Republican policies, insist that we abandon the successful policies and revert to the policies that failed.

Somehow, in the years that have passed since the New Deal, the alchemy of time has transmuted this leaden era of poverty, class bickering and repeated frustration, into a Golden Age in the minds of some people. One might think that the Democratic Party would be grateful to have the New Deal mercifully forgotten. Apparently this is not so. Former President Harry S. Truman was reported on November 20, 1955, to have remarked of a speech by Adlai Stevenson that Stevenson "made the best New Deal speech I ever heard him make." It is plain that the former President still thought that this was just the nicest thing anyone could say about a person.

The answer to our main question, then, is this: the New Deal was not a political philosophy, but a succession of economic, financial, social, labor, agricultural and governmental experiments. Of these experiments, the accomplishments of permanent value in the fields of social insurance, labor legislation and governmental concern for the needy and helpless have been carried on and perfected under the Eisenhower Administration. But the pawnbroker economics, the semiauthoritarian trend in government, the contempt for the states, for the legislative branch and for the Supreme Court, the lack of faith in private enterprise, and the morbid doctrine of the overbuilt economy—all these are the very things the New Republicanism and the overwhelming majority of the American people have decisively rejected.

Hypochondriac Economics

The difference between the New Deal idea and the New Republican idea on how to have a healthy growing economy may be stated metaphorically:

The New Deal view is that the body politic will survive only if it is stimulated, medicated and occasionally amputated.

New Republicanism believes that the body politic has its own internal way of surviving and repairing its ills and bruises, because it is basically healthy.

The difference is between treating the country as if it were an inanimate machine and treating it as a living organism.

If you are tinkering with a machine, you can take off the carburetor and put it back on, but you cannot take a man's hand off and put it back on. You can dope up the fuel that you use in a racing car, but you cannot go on indefinitely shooting a man full of drugs and still have a healthy man. Whenever you tinker with a living organism, you produce reactions throughout the entire organism that may, in many subtle ways, undo the results that you are trying to achieve.

Maybe some people think it would be interesting to see what would happen if, for example, we decreed by law that millions of people throughout the country shall hereafter be paid at least a $1.25 or perhaps (as has been publicly suggested) even $2.00 an hour; or maybe it would be amusing to see what might happen if we poured out the countless billions of dollars that would be required if all of the Opposition proposals in Congress should actually go through. Why not try the legislation, just to see what happens?

That is the kind of attitude which might have been understandable during the depression. There was nothing to lose during the depression. You could try almost anything, however spectacular, and if it didn't work, you weren't much worse off than before, because you couldn't sink much lower. It is quite a different question when you have an economy which is humming along with a stable cost of living, lower taxes, a good degree of prosperity and a reasonable degree of security. You cannot just break in upon this intricate organism, and slash away at it right and left, on the assumption that if you have made a mistake you can always weld it back together again. You cannot weld it. It is a living organism.

John Maynard Keynes once used this figure of speech to illustrate a point about indiscriminate governmental actions

first to loosen the currency and then to tighten it. He said it
was like the mother who first gives her baby castor oil to
loosen him up, and then gives him bismuth to tighten him
up again, and then castor oil again, and then bismuth, and
then castor oil—and pretty soon, said Keynes, you have a
very sick baby.

All this is not to say that the government should do
nothing about the health of our economy. The difference between a healthy man and a hypochondriac is not that the
healthy man ignores his health entirely; rather, he watches
it constantly, and with the earliest signs of trouble he takes
measures in aid of the normal reparative functions of the
body, not in defiance of them. If he is fatigued, he rests—
he does not take Benzedrine. So a wise government will
gently aid the normal economic laws to adjust themselves
when abnormal tendencies begin to develop, by timely moves
in the field of taxation, credit and fiscal policy.

"Down the Road to Socialism?"

It is sometimes said, when another item of social legislation is passed, that we are going "down the road to Socialism." On the other hand, if the government takes some step
to get out of the regulatory field, we are told that we are
going away from Socialism.

The word "Socialism" has become such a general-purpose
epithet that we must begin by making sure we agree on its
meaning. H. W. Fowler, in his *Dictionary of Modern English
Usage,** begins his entry under "Socialism, communism,
anarchism" as follows:

The things are not mutually exclusive; the words are not an
exhaustive threefold division of anything; each stands for a state
of things, or a striving after it, that differs much from that which

* Clarendon Press, Oxford, 1926.

we know; & for many of us, especially those who are comfortably at home in the world as it is, they have consequently come to be the positive, comparative, & superlative, distinguished not in kind but in degree only, of the terms of abuse applicable to those who would disturb our peace.

He then goes on to distinguish the three:

The socialist blames our organization into classes (especially those of capitalists & wage-earners), the communist blames private property, the anarchist blames government as such, for what they all alike find unsatisfactory. The anarchist remedy is to abolish the State & leave all relations between persons & groups to be established & maintained by free contract. The communist's, on the contrary, is, by abolishing all private property, to make the State absolute master of the individual. The socialist's is less simple; he may accept either of the apparently opposite methods of anarchist & communist as being the shortest way to his own end; that is, anarchism & communism are sometimes forms of socialism; or he may be content with something short of communism—not abolishing all property, but transferring the control of public services & the means of large industrial production to the State or the municipality.

Then he adds a statement which is of special significance for our present inquiry about "going down the road":

And further, it is not a case with him (the socialist) as with the others, of all or nothing; abolition of the State or of private property is for them (communists and anarchists) the condition precedent of improvement, & is not to be brought about except by revolution; but, for the socialist, every curtailment of privilege, every nationalization or municipalization of a particular service, is a step forward, worth taking for itself as well as for its contribution to the gradual progress. . . .

An attempt such as this to summarize broad concepts is bound to be oversimplified and debatable, but this statement will serve the purpose of protecting us from going overboard into either of two extreme errors. The first error is that of calling everything Socialist that evidences government concern for the needs of people, no matter how this concern is expressed. There is nothing in the concept of Socialism that gives it any monopoly on, or is particularly relevant to, the theory that the government has a duty to see that such things as good education, disaster relief, pure food and drugs and effective public health services are provided.

The second error is that of supposing that Socialism is not in question until somebody proposes the outright "nationalization of the principal means of production"—which was the classical definition we learned in school. It will not do merely to scoff at those who worry about a gradual movement toward Socialism, by pointing out that no one in this country is seriously proposing the governmental seizure of steel mills and automobile factories. If "every nationalization or municipalization of a particular service is a step forward, worth taking for itself," in Socialist theory, it follows that anyone who proposes any public assumption of a normally private business activity must be prepared to defend himself against the charge of moving in step with Socialism.

This is not true of Communism and anarchism. You do not "go down the road to Communism"; you plunge over the cliff into Communism, or not at all. But you can go down the road to contemporary Socialism, and a number of European countries have taken quite a few brisk strides in that direction, led by parties that frankly call themselves Socialist. These parties are frequently as sincerely anti-Communist as anyone could be, and the animosity is in most cases returned by the Communists, who feel that the Socialists only serve to reduce the head of steam which must build up between extreme left and right to produce the necessary eventual explosion. Once more, we must be on guard against the easy assumption that we can be hospitable toward Socialism for this reason of mutual enmity to Communism. Whether they fight each other or not, both Communists and Socialists believe in measures which are alien to and destructive of what we know to be the sources of our prosperity and freedom.

Why cannot it be said, with all the Eisenhower Administration's forward strides in social legislation, that it too is headed toward Socialism?

We begin with the proposition that a government's concern for the needs of people does not make it Socialistic. The Eisenhower Administration yields to no one—Socialist, Communist, anarchist, New Dealer or Fair Dealer—in its determination that what has to be done to meet the needs of the people will be done.

Having agreed that this objective does not make one a Socialist, we can then proceed to frame a colloquial set of definitions of the Socialist, the reactionary and the New Republican.

A Socialist is a person who, when a job needs to be done for the people, and it can be done by either government or private enterprise, says: "Other things being equal, let the government do it."

A reactionary is a person who, when a job needs to be done for the people, and it cannot be done by private industry, but can only be done by the government, says: "Don't do it at all." He would rather see people go hungry, sick and uneducated than see the federal government enlarge its activity by one iota.

In between these extremes is the view of the New Republicanism and of the vast majority of the American people. We believe that it is wrong for the federal government to get into things, or stay in things, that could be done by individuals or private business. We also believe that it is just as bad for the government, out of a false conception of the limits on its role or out of a craven fear of being mislabeled Socialistic, to refuse to act on behalf of the safety, health, welfare and happiness of its people when the job has got to be done, and no one else can do it.

Let us look at a few contemporary examples of this difference in method.

It is quite possible to have a vigorous federal program in the health field without running the risk of destroying the traditionally private character of our health professions and institutions. For example, there appears to be a good prospect of bringing about privately the kind of insurance pool that will permit the extension of voluntary health insurance to people and risks not now covered. Again, federal medical research programs are being briskly stepped up to hasten the day when some of our worst maladies will be conquered. Grants in aid for public health, the assistance of hospitals and nursing homes and teaching facilities, and a variety of other measures permit the federal government to make a contribution in its proper sphere, without dominating the world of medicine.

Lately a few ultra-Fair-Dealers have begun to show a serious interest in the possibility of providing family allowances in the United States, and a move is on foot to conduct a special study of the Canadian system. The typical family allowance scheme pays a given sum of money per child every week to families with more than a certain number of children. In England, for example, a specified amount is paid for each child beyond the first. This applies even when the breadwinner is earning his full wages. It has nothing whatever to do with wage loss, need or anything else. Millionaires are as much entitled to it as paupers. If you visit England, you can observe on a certain day each week a long queue of women, frequently with perambulators, stretching out from the local post office. These are the wives of Englishmen; they are standing in line to be paid eight shillings and six pence per week per child.

Those who are now suggesting that American husbands likewise send their wives to collect a few dollars a week per child from the government have grossly misjudged the temper and pride of Americans. We prefer to support our own families privately, and we can do it. With average weekly earnings, in manufacturing, of around eighty dollars, we have no need for such charitable concern. Cases of need, or of wage loss, we know how to take care of. But we will not tolerate the idea that America is somehow just one vast settlement house in which *all* the inmates, even when working at full pay, need to have weekly support money from a benign government.

Perhaps the neatest illustration of the American principle that a program to meet the needs of people should be as private and as local as its character will permit is our pattern of wage-loss insurance.

We begin with workmen's compensation. Can its financing be handled by private enterprise? Yes. The risk of industrial injury can be made the subject of accurate actuarial calculation, and private insurers are willing to issue policies against the risk. This being so, we have turned over the great bulk of workmen's compensation to private insurance, with the administration and dispute-settling being handled by the most local possible public agency—the individual state government.

Next comes unemployment compensation. It cannot be financed privately, because unemployment has never been considered an actuarially insurable risk. So, by default, it is turned over to a public agency. But the risk is not so large or long-range that it is beyond the capacity of states to handle, so we leave administration with the states.

Finally we come to old-age and survivors insurance. Once more, we discover that the risk is beyond private business; it is too big, for one thing; it may run up reserves of a hundred billion dollars eventually. Nor can it be handled by the states. The reserves required are too big; people travel back and forth between states for a lifetime; payments must be made to people moving between states for many years; no single state could possibly administer such a system. And so, once more by default, the system must be both public and centralized.

That is really all there is to the matter; we have consciously or unconsciously complied with a very sound and healthy principle, drawn from our instinctive preference for the private and the local way of doing things.

This principle is put to the test—and you can see the sides line up—every time a bill is pending in a legislature or in Congress to provide the latest variety of income insurance: temporary nonoccupational sickness and disability insurance. The ultra-Fair-Dealers want the job taken over by the government and financed by taxes. The New Republicans, however, point out that about two-thirds of the country's employees already have some kind of disability insurance, often more favorable than the proposed statute would provide. To sweep all these plans aside, and substitute a single governmental plan at some uniform low level, is in most cases anything but favorable to the employees affected. Therefore, as in the Eisenhower Administration's plan proposed for the District of Columbia, existing plans are preserved if at least as good as the statutory plan, and employers who do not have such insurance may comply with the statute simply by taking out the appropriate private insurance.

Here again is a risk, like workmen's compensation, that can be handled—and already is handled—through private insurance. Our principle therefore calls for doing the job privately. The fact that it can successfully done privately has already been demonstrated in New York, which has a statute providing for this kind of protection.

On top of the basic system represented by all these plans, which have their genesis in a public statute, we have more recently developed a second layer of benefits in many industries.

The first layer is the bedrock protection afforded by the statutory plan, which may be anywhere from a third to two-thirds of average weekly wages during the period of wage loss.

The second layer is the private supplement, supplied by the employer, or sometimes by the union, in order to bring benefits up to a more comfortable level.

These private benefits have been in existence for many years, but the last ten years have witnessed a phenomenal increase in the number of such plans brought about by collective bargaining.

Supplementation of old-age pension benefits now applies to perhaps twelve million people, and the number is constantly growing.

Supplementation of workmen's compensation is less common, but is becoming a familiar feature of current contracts —particularly since without it the nonoccupational private disability benefits are often higher than the benefits for industrial injury.

The most recent development is the supplementation of unemployment insurance, both as to amount and as to duration in some instances. This is sometimes called the guaranteed annual wage, but is usually an addition to the benefits allowed by unemployment insurance under largely the same conditions.

Not only do these private contracts add a layer of increased benefits to those of existing public plans; they also provide benefits where no corresponding public plan exists, as in the case of nonoccupational disability in most states, hospital and medical expense and the like.

If you add together what we have available in this country under both public and private plans (although they are still seriously deficient in many ways), and compare it with the supposedly more comprehensive plans of other countries, we would probably be found to be as generous in the provision of protection against the exigencies of life as most others, and more generous than many. The reason this is not generally understood, particularly by people from other countries, is that the complete story of our coverage can be found only by searching in many different places, federal, state and private.

And yet, while we have thus provided all these measures for the security of people, the sum total is far from being Socialism. The heavy proportion of private insurance or self-insurance, and the wide dispersion of administration with only a minimum of central control, make it impossible for even the most worried observer to find a real case of Socialism.

All this is what is meant by the remark of the late Frederick Lewis Allen that we have gone, not toward Socialism, but "past Socialism"; for by an entirely different road we have reached a point where our people have even more security and protection than Socialism affords, within our own institutions and freedoms.

To summarize the last two chapters: just as the concept of conservatism has been distorted by reaching back to the ideas of a Europe against which we rebelled, so the word "liberalism" has been tortured out of its true meaning by those who would equate it with the New and Fair Deals.

Historically, liberalism meant belief in freedom. Its prophets were Locke, Hume, Burke, Adam Smith and John Stuart Mill. Its central belief was the liberty of individual persons, and with this went all the corollaries that have been described in this book—private property, free trade, competition, free markets, free prices, rewards for enterprise, noninterference by government, limitation on the powers of the central Executive and decentralization of power as much as possible.

But now the word "liberal" has somehow come to mean in this country someone who believes in New Deal and Fair Deal ideas—concentration of power in Washington, concentration of governmental power in the Executive, administrative discretion in place of rule of law, skepticism of free enterprise and free markets, and preference for government planning over private management.

Therefore, if someone says that the New Republicanism is "liberal," this does not mean it is New Dealish. And if someone says that the New Republicanism is "conservative," this does not mean that it yearns for the days of Louis XIV.

The New Republicanism is liberal in the true sense, and it is conservative in the true sense.

There is no mystery or trick about the reason. The reason is that the principles on which our Republic was founded were thoroughly liberal in this real sense of the word; and therefore the objective of any true American conservative must be to conserve these liberal traditions.

8

Principles of the New Republicanism

The principles of New Republicanism, which give expression and direction to our National Consensus on fundamentals, are these:

1. *We begin by acknowledging reverently the existence of a God of order, justice and love.*

Because this is a universe of order, we may frame our plans around a faith that the innate motivations given us by the Creator will drive us toward progress, prosperity and happiness.

Since this is a universe of justice, then our insistence on the highest standards in government, on a framework of fair play for the settlement of disputes brought on by the free forces of our society, and on the firm and even-handed enforcement of the laws is justified on a higher level than that of good administration; it is justified on the necessity of attuning government to the deepest moral and ethical principles.

And since there is a God of love, our efforts to allay the suffering of the unfortunate, to temper the exercise of raw economic force at the expense of the less strong, and to provide opportunity for each individual person to realize the best that is in himself, are not sentimentalism; they are the governmental counterpart of a rule of life accepted by devout Americans as an expression of their religious convictions.

2. *The individual person is the pre-eminent object of all our political arrangements.*

Governments as such—whether federal, state or municipal —unions as such, business or nonbusiness organizations as such, are only means toward a better life for the person.

This means that in all we do, we must respect his pride, his independence, his right to be himself, his right to come and go as he chooses, and his age-old franchise to work out or fight out his own destiny and keep the rewards of his exertions and ingenuity, so long as he respects the similar rights of others.

It also means that our legislation must deal in separate people as far as possible; we do not deal in classes or masses, and we are not satisfied with statistically average welfare. The well-being of a member of a minority—even a very small minority—is as important as that of the dominant majority, because each member of that small minority is just as much created in God's image as if he happened to be associated with a larger group. God's image is not to be arrived at by drawing a composite portrait using the average features of the majority.

Finally, it means that the person must remain sovereign in his dealings with government. He must not be maneuvered into the position of cringing before it for largesse; he must not be pushed around unnecessarily in his everyday affairs; and he is entitled to have as large a share in government as is administratively feasible.

3. *Government should be as local as possible.*

If the individual is to have as large a share as possible in government, the principle of localism as against centralization follows, since it is axiomatic that a person has a larger say in the running of his school board than in the decisions of the United States Senate.

The convergence of all lines of power in Washington is dangerous, not only because it separates people more widely from their government, but also becaue it has the potentiality of gradually drawing us into the kind of totalitarianism that almost brought a new Dark Age on the world.

State governments must be built up in prestige, strength, fiscal sturdiness and sense of responsibility; and the great municipalities, where most of our people now live, must similarly shoulder an unprecedented share of the over-all job of government.

We believe that the tradition of localization of authority in matters not clearly demanding central concern is fundamental to our federal form of government and to its original wise purpose of keeping a swollen Executive, whether arrogant or beneficent or both, from becoming the master of the people.

4. *Whatever can be done privately should be done privately.*

Even under this principle, and under the principle that government should be as local as possible, there will always be more than enough for the federal government to do, confining itself to matters that neither private entities nor local governments can handle.

But if there is added to the unavoidable federal responsibilities a layer of further jobs that could be managed by states and a still further layer of activities that should be in the hands of private enterprise, the combination is almost certain to inflate the central government to perilous proportions.

Therefore, the government should stay out of business, and when it is necessary to regulate business, it should not cut into the main channel of activity, but simply police the boundaries of the channel to protect the public interest.

5. *The government has a responsibility for prosperity which it discharges best by aiding and releasing, not by overruling, the forces of private enterprise.*

The principle of private enterprise, comprising the ideas of free competition, rewards for incentive, penalties for sloth and opportunity for everyone, is intrinsically right.

The government's principal responsibilities are: to adopt wise tax policies that will stimulate both investment and purchasing power; to battle inflation by striking at its sources rather than by trying to trim off its effects; to attune its own gigantic fiscal movements to the times, so as to aid orderly growth and stability; to use its facilities and resources to help build up areas not sharing in the general prosperity; and to act upon unhealthy turns in the business cycle by guiding the inherent forces of private enterprise, such as credit, rather than by usurping and invading the domain of private enterprise and by affronting and violating its rules.

Dr. Gabriel Hauge, Assistant to President Eisenhower on economic matters, cites a phrase for it: the government should attempt to influence the economic weather and not try to ration raindrops.

6. *The government has a responsibility for enabling working people to improve their lot through fair collective bargaining, which it discharges best by encouraging free*

trade unionism, guaranteeing the right of genuine representative collective bargaining, and then avoiding interference with these free negotiations.

Just as the attitude toward private enterprise stems from a deep faith in the inner soundness of that system, so the attitude toward unionism and collective bargaining is an expression of the fullest faith in those institutions.

Note also the consistency between this policy and the policy of governmental withdrawal from interference with private affairs. Where good unions exist, the government does not have to intervene in the interest of raising labor standards. Where unions are lacking, it sometimes becomes necessary to have minimum wage laws, maximum hours laws and other compulsory laws to eradicate substandard working conditions. The government, therefore, in carrying out its objective of withholding its hand from private matters, is glad to have the job of protecting labor standards more and more taken over by free nongovernmental agencies.

7. *The government has a responsibility for the general welfare of people, which it discharges best by initiating systems of income insurance, disaster relief, aid for education, health, safety and the like, with a maximum of private and local content and a minimum of centralized control.*

It is the objective of New Republicanism to combine a dignified provision against the more serious personal risks inherent in a fast-changing competitive economy with actual strengthening of both individual values and business vigor. It is its objective also to combine the generous marshaling of federal resources in aid of traditionally local activities such as education, roads, health, safety and relief with the building-up rather than the chopping-away of state responsibility and stature.

These combinations are not impossible, but can be achieved only if the determination to achieve them is never for a moment slackened, and if we are willing to apply to the task all the ingenuity, diligence and patience at our disposal. The "easy way" to go at the job of welfare is by abdicating the entire responsibility to a governmental welfare state created by a few strokes of federal legislation. To get comparable benefits—while preserving our American division of function—is "the hard way," but it is our way and it can succeed.

8. *America has its own political philosophy, stemming not from the European left-wing, right-wing concept, but from the ideals of our Revolution and Constitution, and drawing its flexibility and vitality from the American tradition of willingly employing novel mechanisms in changing times to preserve our oldest ideals.*

Our history is one of inventing and applying original and daring devices to spread across a new continent the enduring virtues of personal liberty, equality of opportunity and self-realization of individual persons.

The struggle which formed the basis of our traditions is not that of class against class in a land which has had centuries in which to sort people into aristocrat, gentleman and villein, or in more modern times, into Right and Left; it is rather that of millions of people from every conceivable background fighting side by side against the wilderness, the prairie, the forest, the sea and the forces of nature. The difference is crucial: the former struggle is in essence a contest to divide what is already in hand—mainly a struggle of the have-nots to take away from the haves; the latter struggle is a struggle

to create something where nothing was before, and to produce ever more and more. It is the difference between the
storming of the Bastille, and the California gold rush; it is the
difference between inventing the guillotine and inventing
the reaper; it is the difference between the Corn Laws and
the Homestead Act.

As a result of our people's essentially classless tradition and
sense of similarity of background, it is natural and fitting that
our political scene should display, not a division into left-
wingers and right-wingers, but a large and powerful Center.
A good image of the story of European class conflicts and
left-right struggles is contained in a remark of Martin Luther:
"Mankind is a drunken peasant on a donkey. You heave him
up on one side and he only slides down on the other." But
that is not the pattern for America in the mid-century and
in the critical years ahead. This is no time to harry the American public from crisis to crisis, nor to drive breaches between groups for transient political advantage. The nation
which must shoulder the gravest world responsibilities of the
Thermonuclear Age cannot heave from one side to another
like a drunken peasant on a donkey. Fortunate indeed it is
that the period which assigned us these responsibilities was
also the period in which there appeared the strong, confident,
center-of-the-road American Consensus.

Index

Employment, maximization of, and inflation, 57; in World War II, 46
Employment Act of 1946, 107
Equality of opportunity, 168 ff.
Extremism, and parlor Communists, 15

Facts, and new ideas, 2–8
Fair Deal, 40, 46; see also Ultra-Fair Dealers
"Fair share," labor's, 129–132
Farm, mechanization of, 117; value of, U.S. average, 104
Farm business, distinguishing features of, 93–94
Farm income, and parity price support program, 98
Farm labor force, decline in, 117
Farm price cycles, 105–106
Farm problems, mixed-up approach to, by Democrats, 99–100
Farm program, New Republican, 96 ff.; see also Soil Bank
Farm surpluses, 100
Farm workers, migratory, 121
Farmers, problems of, 94–96
Fascist manifestoes, 13
Federal aid, in local matters, 155; see also Federal government; Federal-state balance
Federal Communications Commission, 64
Federal government, four main internal relations, 8; mistrust of, by Opposition in 1896, 9; responsibility of, for labor standards, 134
Federal grants-in-aid, 28
Federal old-age and survivors' insurance, 77
Federal policies, change in, 6
Federal power, as determined by function, 25; growth of, vs. states' rights, 20–24
Federal Power Commission, 64
Federal procurement, and changes in policies, 6
Federal Reserve Bank discount rate, 42, 54
Federal-state balance, 20–38; division of functions in, 24–26
Federal-state partnership arrangements, 31
Federal-state pattern, emergence of, 26–33
Federal-state system, 162
Federal Trade Commission, 65
Federal workers, fringe benefits, 134–135
Federalist Papers, 13
Flemming, Arthur S., 91
Folsom, Marion B., 91
Food and Drug Laws, 65
Foundations, corporation, 138

Fowler, H. W., 188–189
Free bargaining, 67, 124–129
Free trade union movement, 110
Freedom, ideal of, 168 ff.; loss of, and centralization of power, 33–38
Fringe benefits, 77, 134
Full employment, Opposition policy on, 57–58

"Give-'em-hell" tactics, 8
God, existence of, 198
Government, business of, 67–73; changed attitude toward, 5–6; insistence on highest standards of, 198; local character of, 200; principal responsibilities of, 201–202; welfare of people and, 146–166
Government agencies, acceptance of, 5–6
Government authority, varieties of, 35–36
Government-business balance, 39–109
Government control, optimum amount of, 63–67
Government regulation, 1896 and 1936, 10; and extreme tendencies in business cycle, 39; see also Government control
Government spending, 45, 62
Governors' Conference, 24, 30
Grant-in-aid, federal, 28
Great Plains Program, 104
Green, William, 144
Gross National Product, 1937, 184; 1954–1955, 40, 42
Group insurance, 77
Guaranteed annual wage, 128

Hamilton, Alexander, 171
Happiness, right to pursuit of, 169 ff.
Harper's Magazine, inflation article quoted, 49
Harriman, W. Averell, 17
Hauge, Gabriel, 91, 201–202
Hitler, Adolf, 34
Homestead Act, 171
Hoover Commission, 68
Housing, federal aid to, 155
Human relations, 119
Hume, David, 13, 197
Humphrey, George M., 90
Hydroelectric dams, and power development, 70 ff.
"Hypochondriac" economics, 186-188

Ideas, modern vs. old-fashioned, 2–8
Ideological challenge, 177
Income insurance, 111, 202
Independent parties, 11
Individual freedom, loss of, 33–34
Individual person, pre-eminence of, in Republican political arrangements,

AI

M

M